WHAT I TALK ABOUT WHEN I TALK ABOUT RUNNING

Haruki Murakami was born in Kyoto in 1949 and now lives near Tokyo. His work has been translated into forty-two languages. The most recent of his many honours is the Franz Kafka Prize.

ALSO BY HARUKI MURAKAMI

Fiction

After Dark

After the Quake

Blind Willow, Sleeping Woman

Dance Dance Dance

The Elephant Vanishes

*Hard-Boiled Wonderland and the End of
the World*

Kafka on the Shore

Norwegian Wood

South of the Border, West of the Sun

Sputnik Sweetheart

A Wild Sheep Chase

The Wind-Up Bird Chronicle

Non-fiction

*Underground: The Tokyo Gas Attack and the
Japanese Psyche*

HARUKI MURAKAMI

What I Talk About
When I Talk
About Running

A Memoir

TRANSLATED FROM THE JAPANESE BY
PHILIP GABRIEL

VINTAGE BOOKS
London

Published by Vintage 2009

6 8 10 9 7

First published with the title
Hashiru Koto Ni Tsuite Kataru Toki Ni Boku No Kataru Koto
by Bungeishunjū Ltd., Tokyo, 2007

First published in Great Britain in 2008 by Harvill Secker

Vintage
Random House, 20 Vauxhall Bridge Road,
London, SW1V 2SA

www.vintage-books.co.uk

Photograph on page 181 copyright © Masao Kageyama

Addresses for companies within The Random House Group Limited
can be found at: www.randomhouse.co.uk/offices.htm

The Random House Group Limited Reg. No. 954009

A CIP catalogue record for this book
is available from the British Library

ISBN 9780099526155

The Random House Group Limited supports The Forest
Stewardship Council (FSC), the leading international forest
certification organisation. All our titles that are printed on
Greenpeace approved FSC certified paper carry the FSC logo.
Our paper procurement policy can be found at:
www.rbooks.co.uk/environment

Mixed Sources
Product group from well-managed
forests and other controlled sources
www.fsc.org Cert no. TT-COC-2139
© 1996 Forest Stewardship Council

Printed and bound in Great Britain by
CPI Bookmarque, Croydon CR0 4TD

Foreword

Suffering Is Optional

There's a wise saying that goes like this: A real gentleman never discusses women he's broken up with or how much tax he's paid. Actually, this is a total lie. I just made it up. Sorry! But if there really were such a saying, I think that one more condition for being a gentleman would be keeping quiet about what you do to stay healthy. A gentleman shouldn't go on and on about what he does to stay fit. At least that's how I see it.

As everybody knows, I'm no gentleman, so maybe I shouldn't be worrying about this to begin with, but still, I'm a little hesitant about writing this book. This might come off sounding like a dodge, but this is a book about running, not a treatise on how to be healthy. I'm not trying here to give advice like, "Okay everybody—let's run every day to stay healthy!" Instead, this is a book in which I've gathered my thoughts about what running has meant to me as a person. Just a book in which I ponder various things and think out loud.

Somerset Maugham once wrote that in each shave lies a philosophy. I couldn't agree more. No matter how mundane some action might appear, keep at it long enough and it becomes a contemplative, even meditative act. As a writer, then, and as a runner, I don't find that writing and publishing a book of my own personal thoughts about running makes me stray too far off my usual path. Perhaps I'm just too painstaking a type of person, but I can't grasp much of anything without putting down my thoughts in writing, so I had to actually get my hands working and write these words. Otherwise, I'd never know what running means to me.

Once, I was lying around a hotel room in Paris reading the *International Herald Tribune* when I came across a special article on the marathon. There were interviews with several famous marathon runners, and they were asked what special mantra goes through their head to keep themselves pumped during a race. *An interesting question*, I thought. I was impressed by all the different things these runners think about as they run 26.2 miles. It just goes to show how grueling an event a marathon really is. If you don't keep repeating a mantra of some sort to yourself, you'll never survive.

One runner told of a mantra his older brother, also a runner, had taught him which he's pondered ever since he began running. Here it is: Pain is inevitable. Suffering is optional. Say you're running and you start to think, *Man this hurts, I can't take it anymore.* The *hurt* part is an unavoidable reality, but whether or not you can stand any more is up to the runner himself. This pretty much sums up the most important aspect of marathon running.

It's been some ten years since I first had the idea of a book about running, but the years went by with me trying out one approach after another, never actually settling down to write it. *Running* is sort of a vague theme to begin with, and I found it hard to figure out exactly what I should say about it.

At a certain point, though, I decided that I should just write honestly about what I think and feel about running, and stick to my own style. I figured that was the only way to get going, and I started writing the book, bit by bit, in the summer of 2005, finishing it in the fall of 2006. Other than a few places where I quote from previous writings I've done, the bulk of this book records my thoughts and feelings in real time. One thing I noticed was that writing honestly about running and writing honestly about myself are nearly the same thing. So I suppose it's all right to read this as a kind of memoir centered on the act of running.

Though I wouldn't call any of this *philosophy* per se,

this book does contain a certain amount of what might be dubbed life lessons. They might not amount to much, but they are personal lessons I've learned through actually putting my own body in motion, and thereby discovering that suffering is optional. They may not be lessons you can generalize, but that's because what's presented here is *me*, the kind of person I am.

AUGUST 2007

What I Talk About
When I Talk About Running

One

Who's Going to Laugh at Mick Jagger?

'm on Kauai, in Hawaii, today, Friday, August 5, 2005. It's unbelievably clear and sunny, not a cloud in the sky. As if the concept *clouds* doesn't even exist. I came here at the end of July and, as always, we rented a condo. During the mornings, when it's cool, I sit at my desk, writing all sorts of things. Like now: I'm writing this, a piece on running that I can pretty much compose as I wish. It's summer, so naturally it's hot. Hawaii's been called the island of eternal summer, but since it's in the Northern Hemisphere there are, arguably, four seasons of a sort. Summer is somewhat hotter than winter. I spend a lot of time in Cambridge, Massachusetts, and

3

compared to Cambridge—so muggy and hot with all its bricks and concrete it's like a form of torture—summer in Hawaii is a veritable paradise. No need for an air conditioner here—just leave the window open, and a refreshing breeze blows in. People in Cambridge are always surprised when they hear I'm spending August in Hawaii. "Why would you want to spend summer in a hot place like that?" they invariably ask. But they don't know what it's like. How the constant trade winds from the northeast make summers cool. How happy life is here, where we can enjoy lounging around, reading a book in the shade of trees, or, if the notion strikes us, go down, just as we are, for a dip in the inlet.

Since I arrived in Hawaii I've run about an hour every day, six days a week. It's two and a half months now since I resumed my old lifestyle in which, unless it's totally unavoidable, I run every single day. Today I ran for an hour and ten minutes, listening on my Walkman to two albums by the Lovin' Spoonful—*Daydream* and *Hums of the Lovin' Spoonful*—which I'd recorded on an MD disc.

Right now I'm aiming at increasing the distance I run, so speed is less of an issue. As long as I can run a certain distance, that's all I care about. Sometimes I run fast when I feel like it, but if I increase the pace I shorten the amount of time I run, the point being to let the exhilaration I feel at the end of each run carry over to the next day. This is the same sort of tack I find necessary when writing a novel. I stop every day right at the point where I feel I can write more. Do that, and the next day's work goes surprisingly smoothly. I think Ernest Hemingway did something like that. To keep on going, you have to keep up the rhythm. This is the important thing for long-term projects. Once you set the pace, the rest will follow. The problem is getting the flywheel to spin at a set speed—and to get to that point takes as much concentration and effort as you can manage.

It rained for a short time while I was running, but it was a cooling rain that felt good. A thick cloud blew in from the ocean right over me, and a gentle rain fell for a while, but then, as if it had remembered, "Oh, I've got to do some errands!," it whisked itself away without so much as a glance back. And then the merciless sun was back, scorching the ground. It's a very easy-to-understand weather pattern. Nothing abstruse or am-bivalent about it, not a speck of the metaphoric or the symbolic. On the way I passed a few other joggers, about an equal number of men and women. The ener-getic ones were zipping down the road, slicing through the air like they had robbers at their heels. Others, over-weight, huffed and puffed, their eyes half closed, their shoulders slumped like this was the last thing in the world they wanted to be doing. They looked like maybe a week ago their doctors had told them they have dia-betes and warned them they had to start exercising. I'm somewhere in the middle.

I love listening to the Lovin' Spoonful. Their music is sort of laid-back and never pretentious. Listening to this soothing music brings back a lot of memories of the 1960s. Nothing really special, though. If they were to make a movie about my life (just the thought of which scares me), these would be the scenes they'd leave on the cutting-room floor. "We can leave this episode out," the editor would explain. "It's not bad, but it's sort of ordinary and doesn't amount to much." Those kinds of memories—unpretentious, commonplace. But for me, they're all meaningful and valuable. As each of these memories flits across my mind, I'm sure I unconsciously smile, or give a slight frown. Commonplace they might be, but the accumulation of these memories has led to one result: me. Me here and now, on the north shore of Kauai. Sometimes when I think of life, I feel like a piece of driftwood washed up on shore.

As I run, the trade winds blowing in from the direction of the lighthouse rustle the leaves of the eucalyptus over my head.

I began living in Cambridge, Massachusetts, at the end of May of this year, and running has once again been the mainstay of my daily routine ever since. I'm seriously running now. By *seriously* I mean thirty-six miles a week. In other words, six miles a day, six days a week. It would be better if I ran seven days, but I have to factor in rainy days, and days when work keeps me too busy.

There are some days, too, when frankly I just feel too tired to run. Taking all this into account, I leave one day a week as a day off. So, at thirty-six miles per week, I cover 156 miles every month, which for me is my standard for *serious* running.

In June I followed this plan exactly, running 156 miles on the nose. In July I increased the distance and covered 186 miles. I averaged six miles every day, without taking a single day off. I don't mean I covered precisely six miles every day. If I ran nine miles one day, the next day I'd do only three. (At a jogging pace I generally can cover six miles in an hour.) For me this is most definitely running at a serious level. And since I came to Hawaii I've kept up this pace. It had been far too long since I'd been able to run these distances and keep up this kind of fixed schedule.

There are several reasons why, at a certain point in my life, I stopped running seriously. First of all, my life has been getting busier, and free time is increasingly at a premium. When I was younger it wasn't as if I had as much free time as I wanted, but at least I didn't have as many miscellaneous chores as I do now. I don't know why, but the older you get, the busier you become. Another reason is that I've gotten more interested in triathlons, rather than marathons. Triathlons, of course, involve swimming and cycling in addition to running. The running part isn't a problem for me, but in order to master the other two legs of the event I had to devote a great deal of time to training in swimming and biking. I had to start over from scratch with swimming, relearning the correct form, learning the right biking techniques, and training the necessary muscles. All of this took time and effort, and as a result I had less time to devote to running.

Probably the main reason, though, was that at a certain point I'd simply grown tired of it. I started running in the fall of 1982 and have been running since then for nearly twenty-three years. Over this period I've jogged almost every day, run in at least one marathon every year—twenty-three up till now—and participated in more long-distance races all around the world than I care to count. Long-distance running suits my personality, though, and of all the habits I've acquired over my lifetime I'd have to say this one has been the most helpful, the most meaningful. Running without a break for more than two decades has also made me stronger, both physically and emotionally.

The thing is, I'm not much for team sports. That's just the way I am. Whenever I play soccer or baseball—actually, since becoming an adult this is hardly ever—I never feel comfortable. Maybe it's because I don't have any brothers, but I could never get into the kind of games you play with others. I'm also not very good at one-on-one sports like tennis. I enjoy squash, but generally when it comes to a game against someone, the competitive aspect makes me uncomfortable. And when it comes to martial arts, too, you can count me out.

Don't misunderstand me—I'm not totally uncompetitive. It's just that for some reason I never cared all that much whether I beat others or lost to them. This sentiment remained pretty much unchanged after I grew up. It doesn't matter what field you're talking about—beating somebody else just doesn't do it for me. I'm much more interested in whether I reach the goals that I set for myself, so in this sense long-distance running is the perfect fit for a mindset like mine.

Marathon runners will understand what I mean. We don't really care whether we beat any other particular runner. World-class runners, of course, want to outdo their closest rivals, but for your average, everyday runner, individual rivalry isn't a major issue. I'm sure there are garden-variety runners whose desire to beat a particular rival spurs them on to train harder. But what happens if their rival, for whatever reason, drops out of the competition? Their motivation for running would disappear or at least diminish, and it'd be hard for them to remain runners for long.

Most ordinary runners are motivated by an individual goal, more than anything: namely, a time they want to beat. As long as he can beat that time, a runner will feel he's accomplished what he set out to do, and if he can't, then he'll feel he hasn't. Even if he doesn't break the time he'd hoped for, as long as he has the sense of satisfaction at having done his very best—and, possibly, having made some significant discovery about himself in the process—then that in itself is an accomplishment, a positive feeling he can carry over to the next race.

The same can be said about my profession. In the novelist's profession, as far as I'm concerned, there's no such thing as winning or losing. Maybe numbers of copies sold, awards won, and critics' praise serve as outward standards for accomplishment in literature, but none of them really matter. What's crucial is whether your writing attains the standards you've set for yourself. Failure to reach that bar is not something you can easily explain away. When it comes to other people, you can always come up with a reasonable explanation, but you can't fool yourself. In this sense, writing novels and running full marathons are very much alike. Basically a writer has a quiet, inner motivation, and doesn't seek validation in the outwardly visible.

For me, running is both exercise and a metaphor. Running day after day, piling up the races, bit by bit I raise the bar, and by clearing each level I elevate myself. At least that's why I've put in the effort day after day: to raise my own level. I'm no great runner, by any means. I'm at an ordinary—or perhaps more like mediocre—level. But that's not the point. The point is whether or not I improved over yesterday. In long-distance running the only opponent you have to beat is yourself, the way you used to be.

Since my forties, though, this system of self-assessment has gradually changed. Simply put, I am no longer able to improve my time. I guess it's inevitable, considering my age. At a certain age everybody reaches their physical peak. There are individual differences, but for the most part swimmers hit that watershed in their early twenties, boxers in their late twenties, and baseball players in their mid-thirties. It's something everyone has to go through. Once I asked an ophthalmologist if anyone's ever avoided getting farsighted when they got older. He laughed and said, "I've never met one yet." It's the same thing. (Fortunately, the peak for artists varies considerably. Dostoyevsky, for instance, wrote two of his most profound novels, *The Possessed* and *The Brothers Karamazov*, in the last few years of his life before his death at age sixty. Domenico Scarlatti wrote 555 piano sonatas during his lifetime, most of them when he was between the ages of fifty-seven and sixty-two.)

My peak as a runner came in my late forties. Before then I'd aimed at running a full marathon in three and a half hours, a pace of exactly one kilometer in five minutes, or one mile in eight. Sometimes I broke three and a half hours, sometimes not (more often not). Either way, I was able to steadily run a marathon in more or less that amount of time. Even when I thought I'd totally blown it, I'd still be in under three hours and forty minutes. Even if I hadn't trained so much or wasn't in the best of shape, exceeding four hours was inconceivable. Things continued at that stable plateau for a while, but before long they started to change. I'd train as much as before but found it increasingly hard to break three hours and forty minutes. It was taking me five and a half minutes to run one kilometer, and I was inching closer to the four-hour mark to finish a marathon. Frankly, this was a bit of a shock. What was going on here? I didn't think it was because I was aging. In everyday life I never felt like I was getting physically weaker. But no matter how much I might deny it or try to ignore it, the numbers were retreating, step by step.

Besides, as I said earlier, I'd become more interested in other sports such as triathlons and squash. Just running all the time couldn't be good for me, I'd figured, deciding it would be better to add variety to my routine and develop a more all-around physical regimen. I hired a private swimming coach who started me off with the basics, and I learned how to swim faster and more smoothly than before. My muscles reacted to the new environment, and my physique began noticeably changing. Meanwhile, like the tide going out, my marathon times slowly but surely continued to slow. And I found I didn't enjoy running as much as I used to. A steady fatigue opened up between me and the very notion of running. A sense of disappointment set in that all my hard work wasn't paying off, that there was something obstructing me, like a door that was usually open suddenly slammed in my face. I named this condition *run-ner's blues*. I'll go into more detail later on about what sort of blues this was.

It's been ten years since I last lived in Cambridge (which was from 1993 to 1995, back when Bill Clinton was president). When I saw the Charles River again, a desire to run swept over me. Generally, unless some great change takes place, rivers always look about the same, and the Charles River in particular looked totally unchanged. Time had passed, students had come and gone, I'd aged ten years, and there'd literally been a lot of water under the bridge. But the river has remained unaltered. The water still flows swiftly, and silently, toward Boston Harbor. The water soaks the shoreline, making the summer grasses grow thick, which help feed the waterfowl, and it flows languidly, ceaselessly, under the old bridges, reflecting clouds in summer and bob-bing with floes in winter—and silently heads toward the ocean.

After I had unpacked everything, gone through the red tape involved in moving here, and settled into life in Cambridge, I got down to some serious running again. Breathing in the crisp, bracing, early-morning air, I felt once again the joy of running on familiar ground. The sounds of my footsteps, my breathing and heartbeats, all blended together in a unique polyrhythm. The Charles River is a holy spot for regatta racing, and there is always someone rowing on the river. I like to race them. Most of the time, of course, the boats are faster. But when a single scull is leisurely rowing I can give it a good run for its money.

Maybe because it's the home of the Boston Marathon, Cambridge is full of runners. The jogging path along the Charles goes on forever, and if you wanted to, you could run for hours. The problem is, it's also used by cyclists, so you have to watch out for speeding bikes whizzing past from behind. At various places, too, there are cracks in the pavement you have to make sure you don't trip over, and a couple of long traffic signals you can get stuck at, which can put a kink in your run. Otherwise, it's a wonderful jogging path.

Sometimes when I run, I listen to jazz, but usually it's rock, since its beat is the best accompaniment to the rhythm of running. I prefer the Red Hot Chili Peppers, Gorillaz, and Beck, and oldies like Creedence Clearwater Revival and the Beach Boys. Music with as simple a rhythm as possible. A lot of runners now use iPods, but I prefer the MD player I'm used to. It's a little bigger than an iPod and can't hold nearly as much data, but it works for me. At this point I don't want to mix music and computers. Just like it's not good to mix friends and work, and sex.

As I mentioned, in July I ran 186 miles. It rained two days that month, and I spent two days on the road. And there were quite a few days when the weather was too muggy and hot to run. So all in all, running 186 miles wasn't so bad. Not bad at all. If running 136 miles in a month amounts to serious running, then 186 miles must be *rigorous* running. The farther I ran, the more weight I lost, too. In two and a half months I dropped about seven pounds, and the bit of flab I was starting to see around my stomach disappeared. Picture going to the butcher shop, buying seven pounds of meat, and carrying it home. You get the idea. I had mixed emotions about carrying around that extra weight with me every day. If you live in Boston, Samuel Adams draft beer (Summer Ale) and Dunkin' Donuts are essentials of life. But I discovered to my delight that even these indulgences can be offset by persistent exercise.

It might be a little silly for someone getting to be my age to put this into words, but I just want to make sure I get the facts down clearly: I'm the kind of person who likes to be by himself. To put a finer point on it, I'm the type of person who *doesn't find it painful* to be alone. I find spending an hour or two every day running alone, not speaking to anyone, as well as four or five hours alone at my desk, to be neither difficult nor boring. I've had this tendency ever since I was young, when, given a choice, I much preferred reading books on my own or concentrating on listening to music over being with someone else. I could always think of things to do by myself.

Even so, after I got married at an early age (I was twenty-two) I gradually got used to living with someone else. After I left college I ran a bar, so I learned the importance of being with others and the obvious point that we can't survive on our own. Gradually, then, though perhaps with my own spin on it, through personal experience I discovered how to be sociable. Looking back on that time now, I can see that during my twenties my worldview changed, and I matured. By sticking my nose into all sorts of places, I acquired the practical skills I needed to live. Without those ten tough years I don't think I would have written novels, and even if I'd tried, I wouldn't have been able to. Not that people's personalities change that dramatically. The desire in me to be alone hasn't changed. Which is why the hour or so I spend running, maintaining my own silent, private time, is important to help me keep my mental well-being. When I'm running I don't have to talk to anybody and don't have to listen to anybody. All I need to do is gaze at the scenery passing by. This is a part of my day I can't do without.

I'm often asked what I think about as I run. Usually the people who ask this have never run long distances themselves. I always ponder the question. What exactly *do* I think about when I'm running? I don't have a clue.

On cold days I guess I think a little about how cold it is. And about the heat on hot days. When I'm sad I think a little about sadness. When I'm happy I think a little about happiness. As I mentioned before, random memories come to me too. And occasionally, hardly ever, really, I get an idea to use in a novel. But really as I run, I don't think much of *anything* worth mentioning.

I just run. I run in a void. Or maybe I should put it the other way: I run in order to *acquire* a void. But as you might expect, an occasional thought will slip into this void. People's minds can't be a complete blank. Human beings' emotions are not strong or consistent enough to sustain a vacuum. What I mean is, the kinds of thoughts and ideas that invade my emotions as I run remain subordinate to that void. Lacking content, they are just random thoughts that gather around that central void.

The thoughts that occur to me while I'm running are like clouds in the sky. Clouds of all different sizes. They come and they go, while the sky remains the same sky as always. The clouds are mere guests in the sky that pass away and vanish, leaving behind the sky. The sky both exists and doesn't exist. It has substance and at the same time doesn't. And we merely accept that vast expanse and drink it in.

I'm in my late fifties now. When I was young, I never imagined the twenty-first century would actually come and that, all joking aside, I'd turn fifty. In theory, of course, it was self-evident that someday, if nothing else happened, the twenty-first century would roll around and I'd turn fifty. When I was young, being asked to imagine myself at fifty was as difficult as being asked to imagine, concretely, the world after death. Mick Jagger once boasted that "I'd rather be dead than still singing 'Satisfaction' when I'm forty-five." But now he's over sixty and still singing "Satisfaction." Some people might find this funny, but not me. When he was young, Mick Jagger couldn't imagine himself at forty-five. When I was young, I was the same. Can I laugh at Mick Jagger? No way. I just happen not to be a young rock singer. Nobody remembers what stupid things I might have said back then, so they're not about to quote them back at me. That's the only difference.

And now here I am living in this unimaginable world. It feels really strange, and I can't tell if I'm fortunate or not. Maybe it doesn't matter. For me — and for everybody else, probably — this is my first experience growing old, and the emotions I'm having, too, are all first-time feelings. If it were something I'd experienced before, then I'd be able to understand it more clearly, but this is the first time, so I can't. For now all I can do is put off making any detailed judgments and accept things as they are. Just like I accept the sky, the clouds, and the river. And there's also something kind of comical about it all, something you don't want to discard completely.

As I mentioned before, competing against other people, whether in daily life or in my field of work, is just not the sort of lifestyle I'm after. Forgive me for stating the obvious, but the world is made up of all kinds of people. Other people have their own values to live by, and the same holds true with me. These differences give rise to disagreements, and the combination of these disagreements can give rise to even greater misunderstandings. As a result, sometimes people are unfairly criticized. This goes without saying. It's not much fun to be misunderstood or criticized, but rather a painful experience that hurts people deeply.

As I've gotten older, though, I've gradually come to the realization that this kind of pain and hurt is a necessary part of life. If you think about it, it's precisely because people are different from others that they're able to create their own independent selves. Take me as an example. It's precisely my ability to detect some aspects of a scene that other people can't, to feel differently than others and choose words that differ from theirs, that's allowed me to write stories that are mine alone. And because of this we have the extraordinary situation in which quite a few people read what I've written. So the fact that I'm *me* and no one else is one of my greatest assets. Emotional hurt is the price a person has to pay in order to be independent.

That's what I basically believe, and I've lived my life accordingly. In certain areas of my life, I actively seek out solitude. Especially for someone in my line of work, solitude is, more or less, an inevitable circumstance.

Sometimes, however, this sense of isolation, like acid spilling out of a bottle, can unconsciously eat away at a person's heart and dissolve it. You could see it, too, as a kind of double-edged sword. It protects me, but at the same time steadily cuts away at me from the inside. I think in my own way I'm aware of this danger—probably through experience—and that's why I've had to constantly keep my body in motion, in some cases pushing myself to the limit, in order to heal the loneliness I feel inside and to put it in perspective. Not so much as an intentional act, but as an instinctive reaction.

Let me be more specific.

When I'm criticized unjustly (from my viewpoint, at least), or when someone I'm sure will understand me doesn't, I go running for a little longer than usual. By running longer it's like I can physically exhaust that portion of my discontent. It also makes me realize again how weak I am, how limited my abilities are. I become aware, physically, of these low points. And one of the results of running a little farther than usual is that I become that much stronger. If I'm angry, I direct that anger toward myself. If I have a frustrating experience, I use that to improve myself. That's the way I've always lived. I quietly absorb the things I'm able to, releasing them later, and in as changed a form as possible, as part of the story line in a novel.

I don't think most people would like my personality. There might be a few—*very* few, I would imagine—who are impressed by it, but only rarely would anyone like it. Who in the world could possibly have warm feelings, or something like them, for a person who doesn't compromise, who instead, whenever a problem crops up, locks himself away alone in a closet? But is it ever possible for a professional writer to be liked by people? I have no idea. Maybe somewhere in the world it is. It's hard to generalize. For me, at least, as I've written novels over many years, I just can't picture someone liking me on a personal level. Being disliked by someone, hated and despised, somehow seems more natural. Not that I'm relieved when that happens. Even I'm not happy when someone dislikes me.

But that's another story. Let's get back to running. I've gotten back into a running lifestyle again. I started seriously running and am now rigorously running. What this might mean for me, now that I'm in my late fifties, I don't know yet. But I think it's got to mean *something*. Maybe not anything profound, but there must be significance to it. Anyway, right now I'm running hard. I'll wait till later to think about what it all means. (Putting off thinking about something is one of my specialties, a skill I've honed as I've grown older.) I shine my running shoes, rub some sunscreen on my face and neck, set my watch, and hit the road. With the trade winds wafting against my face, a white heron up above, its legs dutifully aligned as it crosses the sky, and me listening to my old favorite, the Lovin' Spoonful.

As I was running I was struck by a thought: Even if my time in races doesn't improve, there's not much I can do about it. I've gotten older, and time has taken its toll. It's nobody's fault. Those are the rules of the game. Just as a river flows to the sea, growing older and slowing down are just part of the natural scenery, and I've got to accept it. It might not be a very enjoyable process, and what I discover as a result might not be all that pleasant. But what choice do I have, anyway? In my own way, I've enjoyed my life so far, even if I can't say I've *fully* enjoyed it.

I'm not trying to brag or anything—who in the world would brag about something like this?—but I'm not the brightest person. I'm the kind of person who has to experience something physically, actually touch something, before I have a clear sense of it. No matter what it is, unless I see it with my own eyes I'm not convinced. I'm a physical, not intellectual, type of person. Of course I have a certain amount of intelligence—at least I think I do. If I totally lacked that there'd be no way I could write novels. But I'm not the type who operates through pure theory or logic, not the type whose energy source is intellectual speculation. Only when I'm given an actual physical burden and my muscles start to groan (and sometimes scream) does my comprehension meter shoot upward and I'm finally able to grasp something. Needless to say, it takes quite a bit of time, plus effort, to go through each stage, step by step, and arrive at a conclusion. Sometimes it takes too long, and by the time I'm convinced, it's already too late. But what're you going to do? That's the kind of person I am.

As I run I tell myself to think of a river. And clouds. But essentially I'm not thinking of a thing. All I do is keep on running in my own cozy, homemade void, my own nostalgic silence. And this is a pretty wonderful thing. No matter what anybody else says.

TWO

AUGUST 14, 2005 · KAUAI, HAWAII

Tips on Becoming a Running Novelist

t's August 14th, a Sunday. This morning I ran an hour and fifteen minutes, listening to Carla Thomas and Otis Redding on my MD player. In the afternoon I swam 1,400 yards at the pool and in the evening swam at the beach. And after that I had dinner—beer and fish—at the Hanalea Dolphin Restaurant just outside the town of Hanalea. The dish I have is walu, a kind of white fish. They grill it for me over charcoal, and I eat it with soy sauce. The side dish is vegetable kebabs, plus a large salad.

So far in August I've racked up ninety-three miles.

· · ·

It was a long time ago that I first started running on an everyday basis. Specifically, it was the fall of 1982. I was thirty-three then.

Not long before, I'd been running a sort of jazz club near Sendagaya Station. Soon after college—actually I'd been so busy with side jobs I was still a few credits short of graduating and was still officially a student—I opened a small club at the south entrance to Kokubunji Station and ran it for about three years; when they started to rebuild the building I was in, I moved to a new location closer to the center of Tokyo. This new venue wasn't so big, or so small, either. We had a grand piano and just barely enough space to squeeze in a quintet. During the day we served coffee, at night it was a bar. We served pretty decent food, too, and on the weekends featured live performances. This kind of live jazz club was still pretty rare back then, so we gained a steady clientele and the place did all right financially.

Most people I knew had predicted that the bar wouldn't do well. They figured that an establishment run as a kind of hobby wouldn't work out, that somebody like me, who was pretty naive and most likely didn't have the slightest aptitude for running a business, wouldn't be able to make a go of it. Well, their predictions were totally off. To tell the truth, I didn't think I had much aptitude for business either. I just figured, though, that since failure was not an option, I'd have to give it everything I had. My only strength has always been the fact that I work hard and can take a lot physically. I'm more a workhorse than a racehorse. I was raised in a white-collar household, so I didn't know much about entrepreneurship, but fortunately my wife's family ran a business, so her natural intuition was a great help. No matter how great a workhorse I might have been, I never would have been able to make it on my own.

The work itself was hard. I worked from morning till late at night, until I was exhausted. I had all kinds of painful experiences, things I had to rack my brains about, and plenty of disappointments. But I worked like crazy, and I finally began to make enough profit to hire other people to help out. And as I neared the end of my twenties, I was finally able to take a breather. To start the bar I'd borrowed as much as I could from every place that would lend me money, and I'd almost repaid it all. Things were settling down. Up till then, it had been a question of sheer survival, of keeping my head above water, and I didn't have room to think of anything else. I felt like I'd reached the top of some steep staircase and come out to a fairly open place and was confident that because I'd reached it safely, I could handle any future problems that might crop up and I'd survive. I took a deep breath, slowly gazed around me, glanced back at the steps I'd taken here, and began to contemplate the next stage. Turning thirty was just around the corner. I was reaching the age when I couldn't be considered young anymore. And pretty much out of the blue I got the idea to write a novel.

I can pinpoint the exact moment when I first thought I could write a novel. It was around one thirty in the afternoon of April 1, 1978. I was at Jingu Stadium that day, alone in the outfield drinking beer and watching the game. Jingu Stadium was within walking distance of my apartment at the time, and I was a fairly big Yakult Swallows fan. It was a perfectly beautiful spring day, not a cloud in the sky, with a warm breeze blowing. There weren't any benches in the outfield seating back then, just a grassy slope. I was lying on the grass, sipping cold beer, gazing up occasionally at the sky, and leisurely enjoying the game. As usual for the Swallows, the stadium wasn't very crowded. It was the season opener, and they were taking on the Hiroshima Carp at home. I remember that Yasuda was pitching for the Swallows. He was a short, stocky sort of pitcher with a wicked curve. He easily retired the side in the top of the first inning, and in the bottom of the inning the leadoff batter for the Swallows was Dave Hilton, a young American player new to the team. Hilton got a hit down the left field line. The crack of bat meeting ball right on the sweet spot echoed through the stadium. Hilton easily rounded first and pulled up to second. And it was at that exact moment that a thought struck me: *You know what? I could try writing a novel.* I still can remember the wide open sky, the feel of the new grass, the satisfying crack of the bat. Something flew down from the sky at that instant, and whatever it was, I accepted it.

I never had any ambitions to be a novelist. I just had this strong desire to write a novel. No concrete image of what I wanted to write about, just the conviction that if I wrote it now I could come up with something that I'd find convincing. When I thought about sitting down at my desk at home and setting out to write I realized I didn't even own a decent fountain pen. So I went to the Kinokuniya store in Shinjuku and bought a sheaf of manuscript paper and a five-dollar Sailor fountain pen. A small capital investment on my part.

This was in the spring of 1978, and by fall I'd finished a two-hundred-page work handwritten on Japanese man-uscript paper. After I finished it I felt great. I had no idea what to do with the novel once I finished it, but I just sort of let the momentum carry me and sent it in to be con-sidered for a literary magazine's new-writers prize. I shipped it off without making a copy, so it seems I didn't much care if it wasn't selected and vanished forever. This is the work that's published under the title *Hear the Wind Sing*. I was more interested in having finished it than in whether or not it would ever see the light of day.

That fall the perennial underdog Yakult Swallows won the pennant and went on to defeat the Hankyu Braves in the Japan Series. I was really excited and attended several games at Korakuen Stadium. (Nobody ever thought that Yakult would win, so they had already arranged for their home venue, Jingu Stadium, to be used for college baseball.) So I remember that time very clearly. It was a particularly gorgeous autumn, with wonderful sunny weather. The sky was perfectly clear, and the ginkgo trees in front of the Meiji Memorial Gallery were more golden than I'd ever seen them. This was the last fall of my twenties.

By the next spring, when I got a phone call from an editor at *Gunzo* telling me my novel had made the short list, I'd completely forgotten that I'd entered the contest. I'd been so busy with other things. At first I had no idea what he was talking about. But the novel won the prize and was published in the summer. The book was fairly well received. I was thirty, and without really knowing what was going on I suddenly found myself labeled a new, up-and-coming writer. I was pretty surprised, but people who knew me were even more surprised.

After this, while still running my business, I wrote a medium-length second novel, *Pinball, 1973*, and while working on this I wrote a few short stories and translated some short fiction by F. Scott Fitzgerald. Both *Hear the Wind Sing* and *Pinball, 1973* were nominated for the prestigious Akutagawa Prize, for which they were said to be strong contenders, but in the end neither won. To tell the truth, though, I didn't care one way or the other. If I did win it I'd become busy with interviews and writing assignments, and I was afraid this would interfere with running the club.

Every day for three years I ran my jazz club—keeping accounts, checking inventory, scheduling my staff, standing behind the counter myself mixing up cocktails and cooking, closing up in the wee hours of the morning—and only then writing at home at the kitchen table until I got sleepy. I felt like I was living enough for two people's lives. Physically, every day was tough, and writing novels and running a business at the same time made for all sorts of other problems. Running a service-oriented business means you have to accept whoever comes through the door. No matter who comes in, unless they're really awful, you have to greet them with a friendly smile on your face. Thanks to this, though, I met all kinds of offbeat people and had some unusual encounters. Before I began writing, I dutifully, even enthusiastically, absorbed a variety of experiences. For the most part I think I enjoyed these and all the stimuli that they brought.

Gradually, though, I found myself wanting to write a more substantial kind of novel. With the first two, *Hear the Wind Sing* and *Pinball, 1973*, I basically enjoyed the process of writing, but there were parts I wasn't too pleased with. With these first two novels I was only able to write in spurts, snatching bits of time here and there—a half hour here, an hour there—and because I was always tired and felt like I was competing against the clock as I wrote, I was never able to concentrate. With this kind of scattered approach I was able to write some interesting, fresh things, but the result was far from a complex or profound novel. I felt I'd been given a wonderful opportunity to be a novelist—a chance you just don't get every day—and a natural desire sprang up to take it as far as I possibly could and write the kind of novel I'd feel satisfied with. I knew I could write something more large-scale. And after giving it a lot of thought, I decided to close the business for a while and concentrate solely on writing. At this point my income from the jazz club was more than my income as a novelist, a reality I had to resign myself to.

Most people I knew were flat out against my decision, or else had grave doubts about it. "Your business is doing fine now," they said. "Why not just let someone else run it for a time while you go and write your novels?" From the world's viewpoint this makes perfect sense. And most people probably didn't think I'd make it as a professional writer. But I couldn't follow their advice. I'm the kind of person who has to totally commit to whatever I do. I just couldn't do something clever like writing a novel while someone else ran the business. I had to give it everything I had. If I failed, I could accept that. But I knew that if I did things halfheartedly and they didn't work out, I'd always have regrets.

Despite the objections of everybody else, I sold the business and, though a bit embarrassed about it, hung out my sign as a novelist and set out to make a living writing. "I'd just like to be free for two years to write," I explained to my wife. "If it doesn't work out we can always open up another little bar somewhere. I'm still young and we can always start over." "All right," she said. This was in 1981 and we still had a considerable amount of debt, but I figured I'd just do my best and see what happened.

I settled down to write my novel and that fall traveled to Hokkaido for a week to research it. By the following April I'd completed A *Wild Sheep Chase*. I figured it was do or die, so I'd put everything I had into it. This novel was much longer than either of my previous two, larger in scope, and much more story-driven.

When I finished the novel I had a good feeling that I'd created my own writing style. My whole body thrilled at the thought of how wonderful—and how difficult—it is to be able to sit at my desk, not worrying about time, and concentrate on writing. There were untouched veins still dormant within me, I felt, and now I could actually picture myself making a living as a novelist. So in the end the fallback idea of opening a small bar again never materialized. Sometimes, though, even now, I think how nice it would be to run a little bar somewhere.

The editors at *Gunzo*, who were looking for something more mainstream, didn't like A *Wild Sheep Chase* at all, and I recall how unenthusiastic their reception was. It seems like back then (what about now, I wonder) my notion of the novel was pretty unorthodox. Readers, though, seemed to love this new book, and that's what made me happiest. This was the real starting point for me as a novelist. I think if I'd continued writing the kind of instinctual novels I'd completed while running the bar—*Hear the Wind Sing* and *Pinball, 1973*—I would have soon hit a dead end.

A problem arose, though, with my decision to become a professional writer: the question of how to keep physically fit. I tend to gain weight if I don't do anything. Running the bar required hard physical labor every day, and I could keep my weight down, but once I started sitting at my desk all day writing, my energy level gradually declined and I started putting on the pounds. I was smoking too much, too, as I concentrated on my work. Back then I was smoking sixty cigarettes a day. All my fingers were yellow, and my whole body reeked of smoke. *This can't be good for me*, I decided. If I wanted to have a long life as a novelist, I needed to find a way to keep fit and maintain a healthy weight.

Running has a lot of advantages. First of all, you don't need anybody else to do it, and no need for special equipment. You don't have to go to any special place to do it. As long as you have running shoes and a good road you can run to your heart's content. Tennis isn't like that. You have to travel to a tennis court, and you need somebody to play with. Swimming you can do alone, but you still have to go to a pool.

After I closed my bar, I thought I'd change my

lifestyle entirely, so we moved out to Narashino, in Chiba Prefecture. At the time it was pretty rural, and there weren't any decent sports facilities around. But they did have roads. There was a Self-Defense Force base nearby, so they kept the roads well maintained for their vehicles. And luckily there was also a training ground in the neighborhood owned by Nihon University, and if I went early in the morning I could freely use—or perhaps I should say borrow without permission—their track. So I didn't have to think too much about which sport to choose—not that I had much of a choice—when I decided to go running.

Not long after that I also gave up smoking. Giving up smoking was a kind of natural result of running every day. It wasn't easy to quit, but I couldn't very well keep on smoking and continue running. This natural desire *to run even more* became a powerful motivation for me to not go back to smoking, and a great help in overcoming the withdrawal symptoms. Quitting smoking was like a symbolic gesture of farewell to the life I used to lead.

I never disliked long-distance running. When I was at school I never much cared for gym class, and always hated Sports Day. This was because these were forced on me from above. I never could stand being forced to do something I didn't want to do at a time I didn't want to do it. Whenever I was able to do something I liked to do, though, *when* I wanted to do it, and the *way* I wanted to do it, I'd give it everything I had. Since I wasn't that athletic or coordinated, I wasn't good at the kind of sports where things are decided in a flash. Long-distance running and swimming suit my personality better. I was always kind of aware of this, which might explain why I was able to smoothly incorporate running into my daily life.

If you'll allow me to take a slight detour from running, I think I can say the same thing about me and studying. From elementary school up to college I was never interested in things I was forced to study. I told myself it was something that had to be done, so I wasn't a total slacker and was able to go on to college, but never once did I find studying exciting. As a result, though my grades weren't the kind you have to hide from people, I don't have any memory of being praised for getting a good grade or being the best in anything. I only began to enjoy studying *after* I got through the educational system and became a so-called member of society. If something interested me, and I could study it at my own pace and approach it the way I liked, I was pretty efficient at acquiring knowledge and skills. The art of translation is a good example. I learned it on my own, the pay-as-you-go method. It takes a lot of time to acquire a skill this way, and you go through a lot of trial and error, but what you learn sticks with you.

The happiest thing about becoming a professional writer was that I could go to bed early and get up early.

When I was running the bar I often didn't get to sleep until nearly dawn. The bar closed at twelve, but then I had to clean up, go over the receipts, sit and talk, have a drink to relax. Do all that and before you know it, it's three a.m. and sunrise is just around the corner. Often I'd be sitting at my kitchen table, writing, when it would start to get light outside. Naturally, when I finally woke up the sun was already high in the sky.

After I closed the bar and began my life as a novelist, the first thing we—and by *we* I mean my wife and I—did was completely revamp our lifestyle. We decided we'd go to bed soon after it got dark, and wake up with the sun. To our minds this was natural, the kind of life respectable people lived. We'd closed the club, so we also decided that from now on we'd meet with only the people we wanted to see and, as much as possible, get by not seeing those we didn't. We felt that, for a time at least, we could allow ourselves this modest indulgence.

It was a major directional change—from the kind of open life we'd led for seven years, to a more closed life. I think having this sort of open existence for a period was a good thing. I learned a lot of important lessons during that time. It was my real schooling. But you can't keep up that kind of life forever. Just as with school, you enter it, learn something, and then it's time to leave.

So my new, simple, and regular life began. I got up before five a.m. and went to bed before ten p.m. People are at their best at different times of day, but I'm definitely a morning person. That's when I can focus and finish up important work I have to do. Afterward I work out or do other errands that don't take much concentration. At the end of the day I relax and don't do any more work. I read, listen to music, take it easy, and try to go to bed early. This is the pattern I've mostly followed up till today. Thanks to this, I've been able to work efficiently these past twenty-four years. It's a lifestyle, though, that doesn't allow for much nightlife, and sometimes your relationships with other people become problematic. Some people even get mad at you, because they invite you to go somewhere or do something with them and you keep turning them down.

I'm struck by how, except when you're young, you really need to prioritize in life, figuring out in what order you should divide up your time and energy. If you don't get that sort of system set by a certain age, you'll lack focus and your life will be out of balance. I placed the highest priority on the sort of life that lets me focus on writing, not associating with all the people around me. I felt that the indispensable relationship I should build in my life was not with a specific person, but with an unspecified number of readers. As long as I got my day-to-day life set so that each work was an improvement over the last, then many of my readers would welcome whatever life I chose for myself. Shouldn't this be my duty as a novelist, and my top priority? My opinion hasn't changed over the years. I can't see my readers' faces, so in a sense it's a conceptual type of human relationship, but I've consistently considered this invisible, conceptual relationship to be the most important thing in my life.

In other words, you can't please everybody.

Even when I ran my bar I followed the same policy. A lot of customers came to the bar. If one out of ten enjoyed the place and said he'd come again, that was enough. If one out of ten was a repeat customer, then the business would survive. To put it the other way, it didn't matter if nine out of ten didn't like my bar. This realization lifted a weight off my shoulders. Still, I had to make sure that the one person who did like the place *really* liked it. In order to make sure he did, I had to make my philosophy and stance clear-cut, and patiently maintain that stance no matter what. This is what I learned through running a business.

After A *Wild Sheep Chase*, I continued to write with the same attitude I'd developed as a business owner. And with each work the number of my readers increased. What made me happiest was the fact that I had a lot of devoted readers, the one-in-ten repeaters, most of whom were young. They would wait patiently for my next book to appear and grab it and read it as soon as it hit the bookstores. This sort of pattern gradually taking shape was, for me, the ideal, or at least a very comfortable, situation. There's no need to be literature's top runner. I went on writing the kind of things I wanted to write, exactly the way I wanted to write them, and if that allowed me to make a normal living, then I couldn't ask for more. When *Norwegian Wood* sold way more than anticipated, the comfortable position I had was forced to change a bit, but this was quite a bit later.

When I first started running I couldn't run long distances. I could only run for about twenty minutes, or thirty. That much left me panting, my heart pounding, my legs shaky. It was to be expected, though, since I hadn't really exercised for a long time. At first, I was also a little embarrassed to have people in the neighborhood see me running—the same feeling I had upon first seeing the title *novelist* put in parentheses after my name. But as I continued to run, my body started to accept the fact that it was running, and I could gradually increase the distance. I was starting to acquire a runner's form, my breathing became more regular, and my pulse settled down. The main thing was not the speed or distance so much as running every day, without taking a break.

So, like my three meals a day—along with sleeping, housework, and work—running was incorporated into my daily routine. As it became a natural habit, I felt less embarrassed about it. I went to a sports store and purchased running gear and some decent shoes that suited my purpose. I bought a stopwatch, too, and read a beginners' book on running. This is how you become a runner.

Looking back now, I think the most fortunate thing is that I was born with a strong, healthy body. This has made it possible for me to run on a daily basis for almost a quarter century, competing in a number of races along the way. I've never had a time when my legs hurt so much I couldn't run. I don't really stretch much before running, but I've never been injured, never been hurt, and haven't been sick once. I'm no great runner, but I'm definitely a strong runner. That's one of the very few gifts I can be proud of.

The year 1983 rolled around, and I participated for the first time in my life in a road race. It wasn't very long—a 5K—but for the first time I had a number pinned to me, was in a large group of other runners, and heard the official shout out, "On your mark, get set, go!" Afterward I thought, *Hey, that wasn't so bad!* In May I was in a 15K race around Lake Yamanaka, and in June, wanting to test how far I could run, I did laps around the Imperial Palace in Tokyo. I went around seven times, for a total of 22.4 miles, at a fairly decent pace, and didn't feel it was that hard. My legs didn't hurt at all. Maybe I could actually run a marathon, I concluded. It was only later that I found out the hard way that the toughest part of a marathon comes *after* twenty-two miles.

When I look at photos of me taken back then, it's obvious I didn't yet have a runner's physique. I hadn't run enough, hadn't built up the requisite muscles, and my arms were too thin, my legs too skinny. I'm impressed I could run a marathon with a body like that. When you compare me in these photos to the way I am now, they make me look like a completely different person. After years of running, my musculature has changed completely. But even then I could feel physical changes happening every day, which made me really happy. I felt like even though I was past thirty, there were still some possibilities left for me and my body. The more I ran, the more my physical potential was revealed.

I used to tend to gain weight, but around that time my weight stabilized at where it should be. Exercising every day, I naturally reached my ideal weight, and I discovered this helped my performance. Along with this, my diet started to gradually change as well. I began to eat mostly vegetables, with fish as my main source of protein. I never liked meat much anyway, and this aversion became even more pronounced. I cut back on rice and alcohol and began using all natural ingredients. Sweets weren't a problem since I never much cared for them.

As I said, if I don't do anything I tend to put on the pounds. My wife's the opposite, since she can eat as much as she likes (she doesn't eat a lot of them, but can never turn down anything sweet), never exercise, and still not put on any weight. She has no extra fat at all. *Life just isn't fair*, is how it used to strike me. Some people can work their butts off and never get what they're aiming for, while others can get it without any effort at all.

But when I think about it, having the kind of body that easily puts on weight was perhaps a blessing in disguise. In other words, if I don't want to gain weight I have to work out hard every day, watch what I eat, and cut down on indulgences. Life can be tough, but as long as you don't stint on the effort, your metabolism will greatly improve with these habits, and you'll end up much healthier, not to mention stronger. To a certain extent, you can even slow down the effects of aging. But people who naturally keep the weight off no matter what don't need to exercise or watch their diet in order to stay trim. There can't be many of them who would go out of their way to take these troublesome measures when they don't need to. Which is why, in many cases, their physical strength deteriorates as they age. If you don't exercise, your muscles will naturally weaken, as will your bones. Some of my readers may be the kind of people who easily gain weight, but the only way to understand what's really fair is to take a long-range view of things. For the reasons I give above, I think this physical nuisance should be viewed in a positive way, as a blessing. We should consider ourselves lucky that the red light is so clearly visible. Of course, it's not always easy to see things this way.

I think this viewpoint applies as well to the job of the

novelist. Writers who are blessed with inborn talent can freely write novels no matter what they do—or don't do. Like water from a natural spring, the sentences just well up, and with little or no effort these writers can complete a work. Occasionally you'll find someone like that, but, unfortunately, that category wouldn't include me. I haven't spotted any springs nearby. I have to pound the rock with a chisel and dig out a deep hole before I can locate the source of creativity. To write a novel I have to drive myself hard physically and use a lot of time and effort. Every time I begin a new novel, I have to dredge out another new, deep hole. But as I've sustained this kind of life over many years, I've become quite efficient, both technically and physically, at opening a hole in the hard rock and locating a new water vein. So as soon as I notice one water source drying up, I can move on right away to another. If people who rely on a natural spring of talent suddenly find they've exhausted their only source, they're in trouble.

In other words, let's face it: Life is basically unfair. But even in a situation that's unfair, I think it's possible to seek out a kind of fairness. Of course, that might take time and effort. And maybe it won't seem to be worth all that. It's up to each individual to decide whether or not it is.

When I tell people I run every day, some are quite impressed. "You really must have a strong will," they sometimes tell me. Of course, it's nice to be praised like this. A lot better than being disparaged, that's for sure. But I don't think it's merely willpower that makes you able to do something. The world isn't that simple. To tell the truth, I don't even think there's that much correlation between my running every day and whether or not I have a strong will. I think I've been able to run for more than twenty years for a simple reason: It suits me. Or at least because I don't find it all that painful. Human beings naturally continue doing things they like, and they don't continue what they don't like. Admittedly, something close to will does play a small part in that. But no matter how strong a will a person has, no matter how much he may hate to lose, if it's an activity he doesn't really care for, he won't keep it up for long. Even if he did, it wouldn't be good for him.

That's why I've never recommended running to others. I've tried my best never to say something like, *Running is great. Everybody should try it.* If some people have an interest in long-distance running, just leave them be, and they'll start running on their own. If they're not interested in it, no amount of persuasion will make any difference. Marathon running is not a sport for everyone, just as being a novelist isn't a job for everyone. Nobody ever recommended or even desired that I be a novelist—in fact, some tried to stop me. I had the idea to be one, and that's what I did. Likewise, a person doesn't become a runner because someone recommends it. People basically become runners because they're meant to.

Still, some might read this book and say, "Hey, I'm going to give running a try," and then discover they enjoy it. And of course that would be a beautiful thing. As the author of this book I'd be very pleased if that happened. But people have their own individual likes and dislikes. Some people are suited more for marathon running, some for golf, others for gambling. Whenever I see students in gym class all made to run a long distance, I feel sorry for them. Forcing people who have no desire to run, or who aren't physically fit enough, is a kind of pointless torture. I always want to advise teachers not to force all junior and senior high school students to run the same course, but I doubt anybody's going to listen to me. That's what schools are like. The most important thing we ever learn at school is the fact that the most important things can't be learned at school.

No matter how much long-distance running might suit me, of course there are days when I feel kind of lethargic and don't want to run. Actually, it happens a lot. On days like that, I try to think of all kinds of plausible excuses to slough it off. Once, I interviewed the Olympic runner Toshihiko Seko, just after he retired from running and became manager of the S&B company team. I asked him, "Does a runner at your level ever feel like you'd rather not run today, like you don't want to run and would rather just sleep in?" He stared at me and then, in a voice that made it abundantly clear how stupid he thought the question was, replied, "Of course. All the time!"

Now that I look back on it I can see what a dumb question that was. I guess even back then I knew how dumb it was, but I suppose I wanted to hear the answer directly from someone of Seko's caliber. I wanted to know whether, despite being worlds apart in terms of strength, the amount we can exercise, and motivation, when we lace up our running shoes early in the morning we feel exactly the same way. Seko's reply at the time came as a great relief. *In the final analysis we're all the same*, I thought.

Whenever I feel like I don't want to run, I always ask myself the same thing: *You're able to make a living as a novelist, working at home, setting your own hours, so you don't have to commute on a packed train or sit through boring meetings. Don't you realize how fortunate you are?* (Believe me, I do.) *Compared to that, running an hour around the neighborhood is nothing, right?* Whenever I picture packed trains and endless meetings, this gets me motivated all over again and I lace up my running shoes and set off without any qualms. *If I can't manage this much*, I think, *it'll serve me right.* I say this knowing full well that there are lots of people who'd pick riding a crowded train and attending meetings any day over running every day for an hour.

. . .

At any rate, that's how I started running. Thirty-three—
that's how old I was then. Still young enough, though
no longer a *young man*. The age that Jesus Christ died.
The age that Scott Fitzgerald started to go downhill.
That age may be a kind of crossroads in life. That was
the age when I began my life as a runner, and it was my
belated, but real, starting point as a novelist.

Three

Athens in Midsummer—Running
26.2 Miles for the First Time

Yesterday was the last day of August. During this month (thirty-one days), I ran a total of 217 miles.

June   156 miles (36 miles per week)
July   186 miles (43 miles per week)
August   217 miles (50 miles per week)

My goal is the New York City Marathon on November 6. I've had to make some adjustments to prepare for it; so far, so good. I started a set running schedule five months ahead of time, increasing, in stages, the distance I run.

The weather in Kauai in August is wonderful, and I wasn't rained out even once. When it did rain, it was a pleasant shower that cooled down my overheated body. Weather on the north shore of Kauai is generally good in the summer, but it's rare to have such nice weather continue for so long. Thanks to this, I was able to run as much as I wanted. I feel in good shape, so even though I'm gradually increasing the distance I run, my body hasn't complained. These three months I've been able to run pain-free, with no injuries, and without feeling overly tired.

The summer heat didn't wear me down, either. I don't do anything in particular to keep my energy level up during the summer. I guess the only thing I do specifically is try not to drink so many cold drinks. And eat more fruits and vegetables. When it comes to food, Hawaii is the ideal place for me to live in the summer because I can easily get lots of fresh fruits—mangoes, papayas, avocados—literally right across the street. I'm not eating these, though, simply to stave off the summer blahs, but because my body just naturally craves them. Being active every day makes it easier to hear that inner voice.

One other way I keep healthy is by taking a nap. I really nap a lot. Usually I get sleepy right after lunch, plop down on the sofa, and doze off. Thirty minutes later I come wide awake. As soon as I wake up, my body isn't sluggish and my mind is totally clear. This is what they call in southern Europe a siesta. I think I learned this custom when I lived in Italy, but maybe I'm misremembering, since I've always loved taking naps. Anyway, I'm the type of person who, once he gets sleepy, can fall sound asleep anywhere. Definitely a good talent to have if you want to stay healthy, but the problem is I sometimes fall fast asleep in situations where I shouldn't.

I've shed a few pounds, too, and my face looks more toned. It's a nice feeling to see your body going through these changes, though they certainly don't happen as quickly as when I was young. Changes that used to take a month and a half now take three. The amount I can exercise is going downhill, as is the efficiency of the whole process, but what're you going to do? I just have to accept it, and make do with what I can get. One of the realities of life. Plus, I don't think we should judge the value of our lives by how efficient they are. The gym where I work out in Tokyo has a poster that says, "Muscles are hard to get and easy to lose. Fat is easy to get and hard to lose." A painful reality, but a reality all the same.

In this way August waved good-bye (it really did seem like it waved), September rolled around, and my style of training has undergone another transformation. In the three months up till now I was basically trying to rack up the distance, not worrying about anything, but steadily increasing my pace and running as hard as I could. And this helped me build up my overall strength: I got more stamina, built up my muscles, spurred myself on both physically and mentally. The most important task here was to let my body know in no uncertain terms that running this hard is just par for the course. When I say *letting it know in no uncertain terms* I'm speaking figuratively, of course. No matter how much you might command your body to perform, don't count on it to immediately obey. The body is an extremely practical system. You have to let it experience intermittent pain over time, and then the body will get the point. As a result, it will willingly accept (or maybe not) the increased amount of exercise it's made to do. After this, you very gradually increase the upper limit of the amount of exercise you do. Doing it gradually is important so you don't burn out.

Now that it's September and the race is two months away, my training is entering a period of fine-tuning. Through modulated exercise—sometimes long, sometimes short, sometimes soft, sometimes hard—I'm transitioning from *quantity* of exercise to *quality*. The point is to reach the peak of exhaustion about a month before the race, so this is a critical period. In order to make any progress, I have to listen very carefully to feedback from my body.

In August I was able to settle down in one place, Kauai, and train, but in September I'll be taking some long trips, back to Japan and then from Japan to Boston. In Japan I'll be too busy to focus on running the way I have been. I should be able to make up for not running as much, though, by establishing a more efficient training program.

I'd really rather not talk about this—I'd much prefer to hide it away in the back of the closet—but the last time I ran a full marathon it was awful. I've run a lot of races, but never one that ended up so badly.

This race took place in Chiba Prefecture. Up to around the eighteenth mile I was going along at a good enough clip, and I was sure I'd run a decent time. I had plenty of stamina left, so I was positive I could finish the rest of the race with no problem. But just as I was thinking this, my legs suddenly stopped following orders. They began to cramp up, and it got so bad I couldn't run anymore. I tried stretching, but the back of my thighs wouldn't stop trembling, and finally cramped up into this weird knot. I couldn't even stand up, and before I knew it I was squatting down beside the road. I'd had cramps in other races, but as long as I stretched for a while, about five minutes was all it took for my muscles to get back to normal and me to get back in the race. But now no matter how much time passed, the cramps wouldn't go away. At one point I thought it'd gotten better and I began to run again, but sure enough the cramps returned. So the last three miles or so I had to walk. This was the first time I'd ever walked a marathon instead of running. Up till then I'd made it a point of pride that no matter how hard things might get, I never walked. A marathon is a running event, after all, not a walking event. But in that one race, even walking was a problem. The thought crossed my mind a few times that maybe I should give up and hitch a ride on one of the event shuttle buses. *My time was going to be awful anyway*, I thought, *so why not just throw in the towel?* But dropping out was the last thing I wanted to do. I might be reduced to crawling, but I was going to make it to the finish line on my own steam.

Other runners kept passing me, but I limped on, grimacing in pain. The numbers on my digital watch kept mercilessly ticking away. Wind blew in from the ocean, and the sweat on my shirt got cold and felt freezing. This was a winter race, after all. You'd better believe it's cold hobbling down a road with the wind whipping by while you're dressed only in a tank top and shorts. Your body warms up considerably as you run, and you don't feel the cold; I was shocked by how cold it was once I stopped running. But what I felt much more than the cold was wounded pride, and how pitiful I looked tottering down a marathon course. About a mile from the finish line my cramps finally let up and I was able to run again. I slowly jogged for a while until I got back in form, then sped down the home stretch as hard as I could. My time, though, was indeed awful, as predicted.

There are three reasons I failed. Not enough training. Not enough training. And not enough training. That's it in a word. Not enough overall exercise, plus not getting my weight down. Without knowing it, I'd developed a sort of arrogant attitude, convinced that just a fair-to-middling amount of training was enough for me to do a good job. It's pretty thin, the wall separating healthy confidence and unhealthy pride. When I was young, maybe just a fair-to-middling amount of training would have been enough for me to run a marathon. Without driving myself too hard in training, I could have banked on the strength I'd already built up to see me through and run a good time. Sadly, though, I'm no longer young. I'm getting to the age where you really do get only what you pay for.

As I ran this race I felt I never, ever wanted to go through that again. Freeze my butt off and feel miserable? I'll pass. Right then and there I decided that before my next marathon I was going to go back to the basics, start from scratch, and do the very best I could. Train meticulously and rediscover what I was physically capable of. Tighten up all the loose screws, one by one. Do all that and see what happens. These were my thoughts as I dragged my cramped legs through the freezing wind, one runner after another passing me by.

As I've said, I'm not a very competitive type of person. To a certain extent, I figured, it's sometimes hard to avoid losing. Nobody's going to win all the time. On the highway of life you can't always be in the fast lane. Still, I certainly don't want to keep making the same mistakes over and over. Best to learn from my mistakes and put that lesson into practice the next time around. While I still have the ability to do that.

This may be the reason why, while I'm training for my next marathon—the New York City Marathon—I'm also writing this. Bit by bit I'm remembering things that took place when I was a beginning runner more than twenty years ago. Retracing my memories, rereading the simple journal I kept (I'm never able to keep a regular diary for very long, but I've faithfully kept up my runner's journal) and reworking them into essay form, helps me consider the path I've taken and rediscover the feelings I had back then. I do this to both admonish and encourage myself. It's also intended as a wake-up call for the motivation that, somewhere along the line, went dormant. I'm writing, in other words, to put my thoughts in some kind of order. And in hindsight—in the final analysis it's always in hindsight—this may very well end up a kind of memoir that centers on the act of running.

This doesn't mean that what's occupying me at this moment is writing a personal history. I'm much more concerned with the practical question of how I can finish the New York City Marathon two months from now, with a halfway-decent time. The main task before me right now is how I can train in order to accomplish that.

On August 25 the U.S. magazine *Runner's World* came to do a photo shoot on me. A young cameraman named Greg flew in from California and spent the day photographing me. An enthusiastic guy, he'd brought a truckload of equipment by plane all the way to Kauai. The magazine had interviewed me earlier, and the photos were to accompany the interview. There apparently aren't too many novelists who run marathons (there are some, of course, but not many), and the magazine was interested in my life as a "Running Novelist." *Runner's World* is a very popular magazine among American runners, so I imagine a lot of runners will say hi to me when I'm in New York. This made me even more tense, thinking how I'd better not do a lousy job in the marathon.

Let's go back to 1983. A nostalgic era now, back when Duran Duran and Hall and Oates were cranking out the hits.

In July of that year I traveled to Greece and ran by myself from Athens to the town of Marathon. This was the opposite direction of the original battle messenger's course, which started in Marathon and went to Athens. I decided to run it backward because I figured I could start early in the morning from Athens, before rush hour (and before the air grew too polluted), leave the city, and head straight for Marathon, which would help me avoid traffic. This wasn't an official race and I was running all alone, so naturally I couldn't count on anyone to reroute vehicles just for me.

Why did I go all the way to Greece and run twenty-six miles by myself? I'd been asked by a men's magazine to travel to Greece and write a travelogue about the trip. This was an officially organized media tour, sponsored by the Greek government's Board of Tourism. A lot of other magazines also sponsored this tour, which included the typical touristy visits to see ruins, a cruise on the Aegean Sea, etc., but once that was over I'd have an open ticket and could stay as long as I wanted and do as I pleased. This kind of package tour didn't interest me, but I did like the idea of being on my own afterward. Greece is the home of the original marathon course, and I was dying to see it with my own eyes. I figured I should be able to run at least part of it myself. For a beginning runner like me, this would definitely be an exciting experience.

Wait a sec, I thought. *Why just one part? Why not run the* entire *distance?*

When I suggested this to the editors of the magazine, they liked the idea. So I ended up running my first full marathon (or something close to it) quietly, all by myself. No crowds, no tape at the finish line, no hearty cheers from people along the way. None of that. But that was okay, since this was the original marathon course. What more could I ask for?

Actually, if you run straight from Athens to Marathon, it's not quite the length of an official marathon, which is set at 26.2 miles. It's about a mile short. I found out about this years later when I ran in an official race that followed the original course, starting in Marathon and ending in Athens. As those who watched the TV broadcast of the marathon at the Athens Olympics are aware, after the runners leave Marathon, at one point they go off on a side road to the left, run past some less-than-distinguished ruins, and then return to the main road. That's how they make up for the extra distance. At the time, though, I wasn't aware of this, and was under the impression that running straight from Athens to Marathon would be the full 26.2 miles. Actually, it was only twenty-five. But within Athens itself I took a few detours, and since the odometer in the van that accompanied me showed it had driven twenty-six miles, I suppose I ran something pretty close to a full marathon. Not that it matters much at this late date.

It was midsummer in Athens when I ran. As those who've been there know, the heat can be unbelievable. The locals, unless they can't help it, avoid going out in the afternoon. They don't do anything, just keep cool in the shade to conserve their strength. Only once the sun sets do they take to the streets. Just about the only people you see walking outside on a summer afternoon in Greece are tourists. Even dogs just lie down in the shade and don't move a muscle. You have to watch them for a long time before you can figure out whether they're still alive. That's how hot it is. Running twenty-six miles in heat like that is nothing short of an act of madness.

When I told Greeks my plan to run alone from Athens to Marathon, they all said the same thing: "That's insane. No one in their right mind would ever think of it." Before I came, I had no idea how hot the summer is in Athens, so I was pretty easygoing about it. All I had to do was run twenty-six miles, I figured, only worrying about the distance. The temperature never crossed my mind. Once I got to Athens, though, it was so blazing hot I did start to get the jitters. *They're right*, I thought. *You have to be crazy to want to do this.* Still, I'd made this flamboyant gesture, promising I'd run the original marathon course and write an article about it, and I'd flown all the way to Greece to accomplish it. No way could I back out now. I racked my brain to come up with ideas on how to keep from getting exhausted by the heat, and finally got the idea of leaving Athens in the early morning, while it was still dark, and reaching Marathon before the sun was high. The later it got, the hotter it would be. It was turning out to be exactly like the story "Run, Melos!," about a competition to outrun the sun.

The photographer from the magazine, Masao Kageyama, would ride along in the van that accompanied me. He'd take pictures as they drove along. It wasn't a real race, and there weren't any water stations, so I'd occasionally stop to get water from the van. The Greek summer is truly brutal, and I knew I'd have to be careful not to get dehydrated.

"Mr. Murakami," Mr. Kageyama said, surprised as he saw me getting ready to run, "you're not really thinking of running the whole route, are you?"

"Of course I am. That's why I came here."

"Really? But when we do these kinds of projects most people don't go all the way. We just take some photos, and most of them don't finish the whole route. So you really are going to run the entire thing?"

Sometimes the world baffles me. I can't believe that people would really do things like that.

At any rate, I started off my run at five thirty a.m. at the stadium later used in the 2004 Athens Olympics, and set off down the road to Marathon. There's just the one main highway. Once you run roads in Greece you'll understand, but they're paved differently. Instead of gravel, they mix in powdered marble, which makes the road shiny in the sunlight and quite slippery. When it rains you have to be very careful. Even when it isn't raining the soles of your shoes make a squeaky

sound, and your legs can feel how smooth the road surface is.

The following is a shortened form of the article I
wrote for the magazine covering my Athens–Marathon
run.

•

The sun's climbing higher and higher. The road within
the Athens city limits is very hard to run on. It's about
three miles from the stadium to the highway entrance,
and there are way too many stoplights along the way,
which messes up my pace. There are also a lot of places
where construction and double-parked cars block the
road, and I have to step out into the middle of the street.
What with the cars zooming around early in the morning, running here can be dangerous.

The sun starts to come up just as I enter Marathon
Avenue, and the streetlights all go out at once. The time
when the summer sun rules over the earth is swiftly
approaching. People have started to appear at bus stops.
Greeks take a siesta at noon, so they tend to commute to
work pretty early. They all look at me curiously. Can't
imagine many of them have ever seen an Oriental man
running down the pre-dawn streets of Athens before.
Athens isn't the kind of town with many joggers to begin
with.

Four miles into the run I strip off my running shirt

and am naked from the waist up. I always run without a shirt, so it feels great to take it off (though later I'll wind up with a terrible sunburn). Until the eighth mile I'm running up a gradual slope. Hardly a breath of air. When I get to the top of the slope it feels like I've finally left the city. I'm relieved, but at the same time this is where the sidewalk disappears, replaced only by a white line painted along the road, marking off a narrow lane. Rush hour has begun, and the number of cars has increased. Large buses and trucks whiz right by me, at about fifty miles per hour. You do get a vague sense of history with a road named Marathon Avenue, but it's basically just an ordinary commuter highway.

It's at this point that I encounter my first dead dog. A large, brown dog. I don't see any external injuries. It's just laid out in the middle of the road. I figured it's a stray that got hit by a speeding car in the middle of the night. The body still looks warm, so it doesn't seem dead. It looks more like it's just sleeping. The truck drivers zooming past don't give it a glance.

A little further on I run across a cat that's been flattened by a car. The cat is totally flat, like some misshapen pizza, and dried up. It must have been run over quite a while ago.

That's the kind of road I'm talking about.

At this point I really start to wonder why, having flown all the way from Tokyo to this beautiful country, I have to run down this dreary commuter road. There must have been other things I could be doing. The body count for all these poor animals who lost their lives on Marathon Avenue is, on this day, three dogs and eleven cats. I count them all, which is kind of depressing.

I run on and on. The sun reveals all of itself, and with unbelievable speed rises in the sky. I'm dying of thirst. I don't have time to get sweaty, since the air is so dry that perspiration immediately evaporates, leaving behind a layer of white salt. There's the expression *beads of sweat*, but here the sweat disappears before it can even form beads. My whole body starts to sting from the salty residue. When I lick my lips they taste like anchovy paste. I start to dream about an ice-cold beer, one so cold it burns. No beers around, though, so I make do with getting a drink from the editors' van about every three miles or so. I've never drunk so much water while running.

I feel pretty good, though. Lots of energy left. I'm only going at about 70 percent of capacity, but am managing a decent pace. By turns the road goes uphill, then down. Since I'm heading from inland toward the sea, the road is, overall, slightly downhill. I leave behind the city, then the suburbs, and gradually enter a more rural area. As I pass through the small village of Nea Makri, old people sitting at an outdoor café sipping morning coffee from tiny cups silently watch me as I run by. Like they're witnessing a scene from the backwaters of history.

At around seventeen miles there's a slope, and once

over that I catch a glimpse of the Marathon hills. I figure I'm about two-thirds finished with the run. I calculate the split times in my head and figure that at this rate I should be able to finish in three and a half hours. But things don't go that well. After I pass nineteen miles the headwind from the sea starts blowing, and the closer I get to Marathon the harder it blows. The wind is so strong it stings my skin. It feel like if I were to relax at all I'd be blown backward. The faint scent of the sea comes to me as the road gently slopes upward. There is just the one road to Marathon, and it's straight as a ruler. This is the point when I start to feel real exhaustion. No matter how much water I drink, a few minutes later I'm thirsty again. A nice cold beer would be fantastic.

No—forget about beer. And forget about the sun. Forget about the wind. Forget about the article I have to write. Just focus on moving my feet forward, one after the other. That's the only thing that matters.

I pass twenty-two miles. I've never run more than twenty-two miles, so this is terra incognita. On the left is a line of rugged, barren mountains. Who could ever have made them? On the right, an endless row of olive orchards. Everything looks covered in a layer of white dust. And the strong wind from the sea never lets up. What is up with this wind? Why does it have to be this strong?

At around twenty-three miles I start to hate everything. Enough already! My energy has scraped bottom, and I don't want to run anymore. I feel like I'm driving a car on empty. I need a drink, but if I stopped here to drink some water I don't think I could get running again. I'm dying of thirst but lack the strength to even drink water anymore. As these thoughts flit through my mind I gradually start to get angry. Angry at the sheep happily munching grass in an empty lot next to the road, angry at the photographer snapping photos from inside the van. The sound of the shutter grates on my nerves. Who needs this many sheep, anyway? But snapping the shutter is the photographer's job, just as chewing grass is the sheep's, so I don't have any right to complain. Still, the whole thing really bugs me to no end. My skin's starting to rise up in little white heat blisters. This is getting ridiculous. What's *with* this heat, anyway?

I pass the twenty-five-mile mark.

"Just one more mile. Hang in there!" the editor calls out cheerfully from the van. Easy for *you* to say, I want to yell back, but don't. The naked sun is blazing hot. It's only just past nine a.m., but I feel like I'm in an oven. The sweat's getting in my eyes. The salt makes my eyes sting, and for a while I can't see a thing. I wipe away the sweat with my hand, but my hand and face are salty too, and that makes my eyes sting even more.

Beyond the tall summer grasses I can just make out the goal line, the Marathon monument at the entrance to the village of the same name. It appears so abruptly that at first I'm not sure if that's really the goal. I'm happy to see the finish line, no question about it, but the abruptness of it makes me mad for some reason. Since this is the last leg of the run, I want to make a last, desperate effort to run as fast as I can, but my legs have a mind of their own. I've totally forgotten how to move my body. All my muscles feel like they've been shaved away with a rusty plane.

The finish line.

I finally reach the end. Strangely, I have no feeling of accomplishment. The only thing I feel is utter relief that I don't have to run anymore. I use a spigot at a gas station to cool off my overheated body and wash away the salt stuck to me. I'm covered with salt, a veritable human salt field. When the old man at the gas station hears what I've done, he snips off some flowers from a potted plant and presents me with a bouquet. *You did a good job*, he smiles. *Congratulations*. I feel so thankful for these small gestures of kindness from foreigners. Marathon is a small, friendly village, quiet and peaceful. I can't imagine how this was where, several thousand years ago, the Greeks defeated the invading Persian army at the shore in a ghastly battle. I sit at a café in the village and gulp down cold Amstel beer. It tastes fantastic, but not nearly as great as the beer I'd been imagining as I ran. Nothing in the real world is as beautiful as the illusions of a person about to lose consciousness.

The run from Athens to Marathon took me three hours and fifty-one minutes. Not exactly a great time, but at least I was able to run the whole course by myself, my only companions the awful traffic, the unimaginable heat, and my terrible thirst. I guess I should be proud of what I did, but right now I don't care. What makes me happy right now is knowing that I don't have to run another step.

Whew!—I don't have to run anymore.

●

This was my first-ever experience running (nearly) twenty-six miles. And, happily, it was the last time I ever had to run twenty-six miles in such grueling conditions. In December of the same year I ran the Honolulu Marathon in a fairly decent time. Hawaii was hot, but nothing compared to Athens. So Honolulu was my first official full marathon. Ever since then it's been my practice to run one full marathon a year.

Rereading the article I wrote at the time of this run in Greece, I've discovered that after twenty-some years, and as many marathons later, the feelings I have when I run twenty-six miles are the same as back then. Even now, whenever I run a marathon my mind goes through the same exact process. Up to nineteen miles I'm sure I can run a good time, but past twenty-two miles I run out of fuel and start to get upset at everything. And at the end I feel like a car that's run out of gas. But after I finish and some time has passed, I forget all the pain and misery and am already planning how I can run an even better time in the next race. The funny thing is, no matter how much experience I have under my belt, no matter how old I get, it's all just a repeat of what came before.

I think certain types of processes don't allow for any variation. If you have to be part of that process, all you can do is transform — or perhaps distort — yourself through that persistent repetition, and make that process a part of your own personality.

Whew!

Four

SEPTEMBER 19, 2005 · TOKYO

Most of What I Know About Writing
Fiction I Learned by Running Every Day

On September 10 I bid farewell to Kauai and returned to Japan for a two-week stay. Now I'm commuting by car between my office studio in Tokyo and my home in Kanagawa Prefecture. I still keep up my running, but since I haven't been back in Japan for a while there's lots of work waiting to keep me busy, and people to meet. And I have to take care of each and every job. I can't run as freely as I did in August. Instead, when I can grab some free time, I'm trying to run long distances. Since I've been back, I've run thirteen miles twice, and nineteen miles once. So

I've been able, barely, to keep up my quota of averaging six miles per day.

I've also been intentionally training on hills. Near my house is a nice series of slopes with an elevation change equivalent to about a five- or six-story building, and on one run I rounded this loop twenty-one times. This took me an hour and forty-five minutes. It was a terribly muggy day, and it wore me out. The New York City Marathon is a generally flat course, but it goes over seven bridges, most of which are suspension bridges, so the middle sections slope up. I've run the NYC Marathon three times now, and those gradual ups and downs always get my legs more than I expect.

The final leg of this marathon is in Central Park, and right after the park entrance there are some sharp changes in elevation that always slow me down. When I'm out for a morning jog in Central Park, they're just gentle slopes that never give me any trouble, but in the final leg of the marathon, they're like a wall standing there in front of the runner. They mercilessly wrest away from you the last drop of energy you've been saving up. *The finish line's close*, I always tell myself, but by this time I'm running on sheer willpower, and the finish line doesn't seem to get any closer. I'm thirsty, but my stomach doesn't want any more water. This is the point where my legs start to scream.

I'm pretty good at running up slopes, and usually I like a course that has slopes since that's where I can pass other runners. But when it comes to the slopes in Central Park, I'm totally beat. This time I want to enjoy, relatively, the last couple of miles, give them all I've got, and break the tape with a smile on my face. That's one of my goals this time around.

The total amount of running I'm doing might be going down, but at least I'm following one of my basic rules for training: I never take two days off in a row. Muscles are like work animals that are quick on the uptake. If you carefully increase the load, step by step, they learn to take it. As long as you explain your expectations to them by actually showing them examples of the amount of work they have to endure, your muscles will comply and gradually get stronger. It doesn't happen overnight, of course. But as long as you take your time and do it in stages, they won't complain—aside from the occasional long face—and they'll very patiently and obediently grow stronger. Through repetition you input into your muscles the message that this is how much work they have to perform. Our muscles are very conscientious. As long as we observe the correct procedure, they won't complain.

If, however, the load halts for a few days, the muscles automatically assume they don't have to work that hard anymore, and they lower their limits. Muscles really are like animals, and they want to take it as easy as possible; if pressure isn't applied to them, they relax and cancel out the memory of all that work. Input this canceled memory once again, and you have to repeat the whole journey from the very beginning. Naturally it's important to take a break sometimes, but in a critical time like this, when I'm training for a race, I have to show my muscles who's boss. I have to make it clear to them what's expected. I have to maintain a certain tension by being unsparing, but not to the point where I burn out. These are tactics that all experienced runners learn over time.

While I've been in Japan a new short-story collection of mine, *Strange Tales from Tokyo*, has come out, and I have to do several interviews about the book. I also have to check the galleys for a book of music criticism that's coming out in November and meet with people to discuss the cover. Then I have to go over my old translations of Raymond Carver's complete works. With new paperback editions of these coming out, I want to revise all the translations, which is time consuming. On top of this, I have to write a long introduction to the short-story collection *Blind Willow, Sleeping Woman*, which will be published next year in the U.S. Plus I'm steadily working on these essays on running, though nobody in particular has asked me to. Just like a silent village blacksmith, tinkering away.

There are also a few business details I have to take care of. While we were living in the States, the woman who works in our Tokyo office as our assistant all of a sudden announced that she's getting married at the beginning of next year and wants to quit, so we have to look for a replacement. Can't have the office shut down over the summer. And soon after I return to Cambridge I have to give a few lectures at the university, so I've got to prepare for them as well.

So I try, in the short amount of time I have, to take care of all these things as best I can. And I have to keep up my running to prepare for the NYC Marathon. Even if there were two of me, I still couldn't do all that has to be done. No matter what, though, I keep up my running. Running every day is a kind of lifeline for me, so I'm not going to lay off or quit just because I'm busy. If I used being busy as an excuse not to run, I'd never run again. I have only a few reasons to keep on running, and a truckload of them to quit. All I can do is keep those *few reasons* nicely polished.

Usually when I'm in Tokyo I run around the Jingu Gaien, the outer gardens of the Meiji Shrine, a course that passes Jingu Stadium. It doesn't compare with Central Park in New York City, but it's one of the few places in Tokyo with any greenery. I've run this course for years and have a clear sense of the distance. I've memorized all the holes and bumps along the way, so it's the perfect place to practice and get a sense of how fast I'm going. Unfortunately there's a lot of traffic in the area, not to mention pedestrians, and depending on the time of day the air isn't so clean—but it's in the middle of Tokyo, so that's to be expected. It's the best I can ask for. I consider myself fortunate to have a place to run so close to my apartment.

One lap around Jingu Gaien is a little more than three-quarters of a mile, and I like the fact that they have distance markers in the ground. Whenever I want to run a set speed—a nine-minute-mile pace, or eight-minute, or seven-and-a-half—I run this course. When I first started to run the Jingu Gaien course, Toshihiko Seko was still an active runner and he used this course too. He was training hard in preparation for the Los Angeles Olympics. A shiny gold medal was the only thing on his mind. He'd lost the chance to go to the Moscow Olympics because of the boycott, so Los Angeles was perhaps his last chance to win a medal. There was a kind of heroic air about him, something you could see clearly in his eyes. Nakamura, the manager of the S&B team, was still alive and well back then, and the team had a string of top-notch runners and was at the height of its power. The S&B team used this course every day for training, and over time we naturally grew to know each other by sight. Once I even traveled to Okinawa to write an article on them while they were training there.

Each of these runners would jog individually early in the morning before going to work, and then in the afternoon the team would work out together. Back then I used to jog there before seven a.m.—when the traffic wasn't bad, there weren't as many pedestrians, and the air was relatively clean—and the S&B team members and I would often pass each other and nod a greeting. On rainy days we'd exchange a smile, a guess-we're-both-having-it-tough kind of smile. I remember two young runners in particular, Taniguchi and Kanei. They were both in their late twenties, both former members of the Waseda University track team, where they'd been standouts in the Hakone relay race. After Seko was named manager of the S&B team, they were expected to be the two young stars of the team. They were the caliber of runner expected to win medals at the Olympics someday, and hard training didn't faze them. Sadly, though, they were killed in a car accident when the team was training together in Hokkaido in the summer. I'd seen with my own eyes the tough regimen they'd put themselves through, and it was a real shock when I heard the news of their deaths. It hurt me to hear this, and I felt it was a terrible waste.

We'd hardly ever spoken, and I didn't know them personally that well. I only learned after their deaths that they had both just gotten married. Still, as a fellow long-distance runner who'd encountered them day after day, I felt like we somehow understood each other. Even if the skill level varies, there are things that only runners understand and share. I truly believe that.

Even now, when I run along Jingu Gaien or Akasaka Gosho, sometimes I remember these other runners. I'll round a corner and feel like I should see them coming toward me, silently running, their breath white in the morning air. And I always think this: They put up with such strenuous training, and where did their thoughts, their hopes and dreams, disappear to? When people pass away, do their thoughts just vanish?

Around my home in Kanagawa I can do a completely different type of training. As I mentioned before, near my house is a running course with lots of steep slopes. There's also another course nearby that takes about three hours to complete—perfect for a long run. Most of it is a flat road that parallels a river and the sea, and there aren't many cars and hardly any traffic lights to slow me up. The air is clean, too, unlike in Tokyo. It can get a little boring to run by yourself for three hours, but I listen to music, and since I know what I'm up against I can enjoy the run. The only problem is that it's a course where you loop back halfway, so you can't just quit in the middle if you get tired. I have to make it back on my own steam even if it means crawling. Overall, though, it's a nice environment to train in.

Back to novels for a moment.

In every interview I'm asked what's the most important quality a novelist has to have. It's pretty obvious: talent. No matter how much enthusiasm and effort you put into writing, if you totally lack literary talent you can forget about being a novelist. This is more of a pre-requisite than a necessary quality. If you don't have any fuel, even the best car won't run.

The problem with talent, though, is that in most cases the person involved can't control its amount or quality. You might find the amount isn't enough and you want to increase it, or you might try to be frugal to make it last longer, but in neither case do things work out that easily. Talent has a mind of its own and wells up when it wants to, and once it dries up, that's it. Of course certain poets and rock singers whose genius went out in a blaze of glory—people like Schubert and Mozart, whose dramatic early deaths turned them into legends—have a certain appeal, but for the vast majority of us this isn't the model we follow.

If I'm asked what the next most important quality is for a novelist, that's easy too: focus—the ability to concentrate all your limited talents on whatever's critical at the moment. Without that you can't accomplish anything of value, while, if you can focus effectively, you'll be able to compensate for an erratic talent or even a shortage of it. I generally concentrate on work for three or four hours every morning. I sit at my desk and focus totally on what I'm writing. I don't see anything else, I don't think about anything else. Even a novelist who has a lot of talent and a mind full of great new ideas probably can't write a thing if, for instance, he's suffering a lot of pain from a cavity. The pain blocks concentration.

That's what I mean when I say that without focus you can't accomplish anything.

After focus, the next most important thing for a novelist is, hands down, endurance. If you concentrate on writing three or four hours a day and feel tired after a week of this, you're not going to be able to write a long work. What's needed for a writer of fiction—at least one who hopes to write a novel—is the energy to focus every day for half a year, or a year, two years. You can compare it to breathing. If concentration is the process of just holding your breath, endurance is the art of slowly, quietly breathing at the same time you're storing air in your lungs. Unless you can find a balance between both, it'll be difficult to write novels professionally over a long time. Continuing to breathe while you hold your breath.

Fortunately, these two disciplines—focus and endurance—are different from talent, since they can be acquired and sharpened through training. You'll naturally learn both concentration and endurance when you sit down every day at your desk and train yourself to focus on one point. This is a lot like the training of muscles I wrote of a moment ago. You have to continually transmit the object of your focus to your entire body, and make sure it thoroughly assimilates the information necessary for you to write every single day and concentrate on the work at hand. And gradually you'll expand the limits of what you're able to do. Almost imperceptibly you'll make the bar rise. This involves the same process as jogging every day to strengthen your muscles and develop a runner's physique. Add a stimulus and keep it up. And repeat. Patience is a must in this process, but I guarantee the results will come.

In private correspondence the great mystery writer Raymond Chandler once confessed that even if he didn't write anything, he made sure he sat down at his desk every single day and concentrated. I understand the purpose behind his doing this. This is the way Chandler gave himself the physical stamina a professional writer needs, quietly strengthening his willpower. This sort of daily training was indispensable to him.

Writing novels, to me, is basically a kind of manual labor. Writing itself is mental labor, but finishing an entire book is closer to manual labor. It doesn't involve heavy lifting, running fast, or leaping high. Most people, though, only see the surface reality of writing and think of writers as involved in quiet, intellectual work done in their study. If you have the strength to lift a coffee cup, they figure, you can write a novel. But once you try your hand at it, you soon find that it isn't as peaceful a job as it seems. The whole process—sitting at your desk, focusing your mind like a laser beam, imagining something out of a blank horizon, creating a story, selecting the right words, one by one, keeping the whole flow of the story on track—requires far more energy, over a long period, than most people ever imagine. You might not move your body around, but there's grueling, dynamic labor going on inside you. Everybody uses their mind when they think. But a writer puts on an outfit called narrative and thinks with his entire being; and for the novelist that process requires putting into play all your physical reserve, often to the point of overexertion.

Writers blessed with talent to spare go through this process unconsciously, in some cases oblivious to it. Especially when they're young, as long as they have a certain level of talent it's not so difficult for them to write a novel. They easily clear all kinds of hurdles. Being young means your whole body is filled with a natural vitality. Focus and endurance appear as needed, and you never need to seek them on your own. If you're young and talented, it's like you have wings.

In most cases, though, as youth fades, that sort of free-form vigor loses its natural vitality and brilliance. After you pass a certain age, things you were able to do easily aren't so easy anymore—just as a fastball pitcher's speed starts to slip away with time. Of course, it's possible for people as they mature to make up for a decline in natural talent. Like when a fastball pitcher transforms himself into a cleverer pitcher who relies on changeups. But there is a limit. And there definitely is a sense of loss.

On the other hand, writers who aren't blessed with much talent—those who barely make the grade—need to build up their strength at their own expense. They have to train themselves to improve their focus, to increase their endurance. To a certain extent they're forced to make these qualities stand in for talent. And while they're getting by on these, they may actually discover real, hidden talent within them. They're sweating, digging out a hole at their feet with a shovel, when they run across a deep, secret water vein. It's a lucky thing, but what made this good fortune possible was all the training they did that gave them the strength to keep on digging. I imagine that late-blooming writers have all gone through a similar process.

Naturally there are people in the world (only a handful, for sure) blessed with enormous talent that, from beginning to end, doesn't fade, and whose works are always of the highest quality. These fortunate few have a water vein that never dries up, no matter how much they tap into it. For literature, this is something to be thankful for. It's hard to imagine the history of literature without such figures as Shakespeare, Balzac, and Dickens. But the giants are, in the end, giants—exceptional, legendary figures. The remaining majority of writers who can't reach such heights (including me, of course) have to supplement what's missing from their store of talent through whatever means they can. Otherwise it's impossible for them to keep on writing novels of any value. The methods and directions a writer takes in order to supplement himself becomes part of that writer's individuality, what makes him special.

Most of what I know about writing I've learned

through running every day. These are practical, physical lessons. How much can I push myself? How much rest is appropriate—and how much is too much? How far can I take something and still keep it decent and consistent? When does it become narrow-minded and inflexible? How much should I be aware of the world outside, and how much should I focus on my inner world? To what extent should I be confident in my abilities, and when should I start doubting myself? I know that if I hadn't become a long-distance runner when I became a novelist, my work would have been vastly different. How different? Hard to say. But something would have definitely been different.

In any event, I'm happy I haven't stopped running all these years. The reason is, I like the novels I've written. And I'm really looking forward to seeing what kind of novel I'll produce next. Since I'm a writer with limits—an imperfect person living an imperfect, limited life—the fact that I can still feel this way is a real accomplishment. Calling it a miracle might be an exaggeration, but I really do feel this way. And if running every day helps me accomplish this, then I'm very grateful to running.

People sometimes sneer at those who run every day, claiming they'll go to any length to live longer. But I don't think that's the reason most people run. Most runners run not because they want to live longer, but because they want to live life to the fullest. If you're going to while away the years, it's far better to live them with clear goals and fully alive than in a fog, and I believe running helps you do that. Exerting yourself to the fullest within your individual limits: that's the essence of running, and a metaphor for life—and for me, for writing as well. I believe many runners would agree.

I'm going to a gym near my place in Tokyo to get a massage. What the trainer does is less a massage than a routine to help me stretch muscles I can't stretch well alone. All my hard training has made them stiff, and if I don't get this kind of massage my body might fall apart right before the race. It's important to push your body to its limits, but exceed those and the whole thing's a waste.

The trainer who massages me is a young woman, but she's strong. Her massage is very—or maybe I should say *extremely*—painful. After a half-hour massage, my clothes, down to my underwear, are soaked. The trainer is always amazed at my condition. "You really let your muscles get too tight," she says. "They're ready to cramp up. Most people would have had cramps long ago. I'm really surprised you can live like this."

If I continue to overwork my muscles, she warns, sooner or later something's going to give. She might be right. But I also have a feeling—a hope—that she isn't, because I've been pushing my muscles to the limits like this for a long time. Whenever I focus on training, my muscles get tight. When I put on my jogging shoes in the morning and set out, my feet are so heavy it feels like I'll never get them moving. I start running down the road, slowly, almost dragging my feet. An old lady from the neighborhood is walking quickly down the street, and I can't even pass her. But as I keep on running, my muscles gradually loosen up, and after about twenty minutes I'm able to run normally. I start to speed up. After this I can run mechanically, without any problem.

In other words, my muscles are the type that need a long time to warm up. They're slow to get started. But once they're warmed up they can keep working well for a long time with no strain. They're the kind of muscles you need for long distances, but aren't at all suited for short distances. In a short-distance event, by the time my engine started to rev up the race would already be over. I don't know any technical details about the characteristics of this type of muscle, but I imagine it's mostly innate. And I feel that this type of muscle is connected to the way my mind works. What I mean is, a person's mind is controlled by his body, right? Or is it the opposite—the way your mind works influences the structure of the body? Or do the body and mind closely influence each other and act on each other? What I do know is that people have certain inborn tendencies, and whether a person likes them or not, they're inescapable. Tendencies can be adjusted, to a degree, but their essence can never be changed.

The same goes for the heart. My pulse is generally around fifty beats per minute, which I think is pretty slow. (By the way, I heard that the gold medalist at the Sydney Olympics, Naoko Takahashi, has a pulse of thirty-five.) But if I run for about thirty minutes it rises to about seventy. After I run as hard as I can it gets near one hundred. So it's only after running that my pulse gets up to the level of most people's resting rate. This is also a facet of a long-distance type of constitution. After I started running, my resting pulse rate went down noticeably. My heart had adjusted its rate to suit the function of long-distance running. If it were high at rest and got higher as I ran, my body would break down. In America whenever a nurse takes my pulse, she invariably says, "Ah, you must be a runner." I imagine most long-distance runners who have run a long time have had a similar experience. When you see runners in town it's easy to distinguish beginners from veterans. The ones panting are beginners; the ones with quiet, measured breathing are the veterans. Their hearts, lost in thought, slowly tick away time. When we pass each other on the road, we listen to the rhythm of each other's breathing, and sense the way the other person is ticking away the moments. Much like two writers perceive each other's diction and style.

So anyway, my muscles right now are really tight, and stretching doesn't loosen them up. I'm peaking in terms of training, but even so they're tighter than usual. Sometimes I have to hit my legs with a fist when they get tight to loosen them up. (Yes, it hurts.) My muscles can be as stubborn as—or more stubborn than—I am. They remember things and endure, and to some extent they improve. But they never compromise. They don't give up. This is my body, with all its limits and quirks. Just as with my face, even if I don't like it it's the only one I get, so I've got to make do. As I've grown older, I've naturally come to terms with this. You open the fridge and can make a nice—actually even a pretty smart—meal with the leftovers. All that's left is an apple, an onion, cheese, and eggs, but you don't complain. You make do with what you have. As you age you learn even to be happy with what you have. That's one of the few good points of growing older.

It's been a while since I've run the streets of Tokyo, which in September is still sweltering. The lingering heat of the summer in the city is something else. I silently run, my whole body sweaty. I can feel even my cap steadily getting soaked. The sweat is part of my clear shadow as it drips onto the ground. The drops of sweat hit the pavement and immediately evaporate.

No matter where you go, the expressions on the faces of long-distance runners are all the same. They all look like they're thinking about something as they run. They might not be thinking about anything at all, but they look like they're intently thinking. It's amazing that

they're all running in heat like this. But, come to think
of it, so am I.

As I run the Jingu Gaien course a woman I pass calls
out to me. One of my readers, it turns out. This doesn't
happen very often, but sometimes it does. I stop and we
talk for a minute. "I've been reading your novels for over
twenty years," she tells me. She began in her late teens
and is now in her late thirties. "Thank you," I tell her.
We both smile, shake hands, and say good-bye. I'm
afraid my hand must have been pretty sweaty. I continue
running, and she walks off to her destination, wherever
that is. And I continue running toward my destination.
And where is that? New York, of course.

Five

Even If I Had a Long Ponytail Back Then

In the Boston area every summer there are a few days so unpleasant you feel like cursing everything in sight. If you can get through those, though, it's not bad the rest of the time. The rich escape the heat by going to Vermont or Cape Cod, which leaves the city nice and empty. The trees that line the walking path along the river provide plenty of cool shade, and Harvard and Boston University students are always out on the glittering river practicing for a regatta. Young girls in revealing bikinis are sunbathing on beach towels, listening to their Walkmen or iPods. An ice cream van stops and sets up shop. Someone's playing a guitar, an old

Neil Young tune, and a long-haired dog is single-mindedly chasing a Frisbee. A Democrat psychiatrist (at least that's who I imagine he is) drives along the river road in a russet-colored Saab convertible.

The special New England fall—short and lovely—fades in and out, and finally settles in. Little by little the deep, overwhelming green that surrounds us gives way to a faint yellow. By the time I need to wear sweatpants over my running shorts, dead leaves are swirling in the wind and acorns are hitting the asphalt with a hard, dry crack. Industrious squirrels are running around like crazy trying to gather up enough provisions to last them through the winter.

Once Halloween is over, winter, like some capable tax collector, sets in, concisely and silently. Before I realize it the river is covered in thick ice and the boats have disappeared. If you wanted to, you could walk across the river to the other side. The trees are barren of leaves, and the thin branches scrape against each other in the wind, rattling like dried-up bones. Way up in the trees you can catch a glimpse of squirrels' nests. The squirrels must be fast asleep inside, dreaming. Flocks of geese fly down from Canada, reminding me that it's even colder north of here. The wind blowing across the river is as cold and sharp as a newly honed hatchet. The days get shorter and shorter, the clouds thicker.

We runners wear gloves, wool caps pulled down to

our ears, and face masks. Still, our fingertips freeze and our earlobes sting. If it's just the cold wind, that's all right. If we think we can put up with it, somehow we can. The fatal blow comes when there's a snowstorm. During the night the snow freezes into giant slippery mounds of ice, making the roads impassable. So we give up on running and instead try to keep in shape by swimming in indoor pools, pedaling away on those worthless bicycling machines, waiting for spring to come.

The river I'm talking about is the Charles River. People enjoy being around the river. Some take leisurely walks, walk their dogs, or bicycle or jog, while others enjoy rollerblading. (How such a dangerous pastime can be enjoyable, I frankly can't fathom.) As if pulled in by a magnet, people gather on the banks of the river.

Seeing a lot of water like that every day is probably an important thing for human beings. *For human beings* might be a bit of a generalization—but I do know it's important for one person: me. If I go for a time without seeing water, I feel like something's slowly draining out of me. It's probably like the feeling a music lover has when, for whatever reason, he's separated from music for a long time. The fact that I was raised near the sea might have something to do with it.

The surface of the water changes from day to day: the color, the shape of the waves, the speed of the current. Each season brings distinct changes to the plants and animals that surround the river. Clouds of all sizes show up and move on, and the surface of the river, lit by the sun, reflects these white shapes as they come and go, sometimes faithfully, sometimes distortedly. Whenever the seasons change, the direction of the wind fluctuates like someone threw a switch. And runners can detect each notch in the seasonal shift in the feel of the wind against our skin, its smell and direction. In the midst of this flow, I'm aware of myself as one tiny piece in the gigantic mosaic of nature. I'm just a replaceable natural phenomenon, like the water in the river that flows under the bridge toward the sea.

In March the hard snow finally melts, and after the uncomfortable slush following the thaw has dried — around the time people start to remove their heavy coats and head out to the Charles River, where the cherry blossoms along the riverside will soon appear — I begin to feel like the stage is set, finally, because the Boston Marathon is just around the corner.

Right now, though, it's just the beginning of October. It's starting to feel a bit too cold to run in a tank top, but still too early to wear a long-sleeved shirt. It's just over a month until the New York City Marathon. About time I cut back on the mileage and get rid of the exhaustion I've built up. Time to start tapering off. No matter how far I run from now on, it won't help me in the race. In fact, it might actually hurt my chances.

Looking back at my running log, I think I've been able to prepare for the race at a decent pace:

June	156 miles
July	186 miles
August	217 miles
September	186 miles

The log forms a nice pyramid. The weekly distance averages out in June to thirty-six miles, then forty-three miles, then fifty, then back to forty-three. I expect that October will be about the same as June, roughly thirty-six miles per week.

I also bought some new Mizuno running shoes. At City Sports in Cambridge I tried on all kinds of models, but ended up buying the same Mizunos I've been practicing in. They're light, and the cushioning of the sole is a little hard. As always, they take a while to get used to. I like the fact that this brand of shoes doesn't have any extra bells and whistles. This is just my personal preference, nothing more. Each person has his own likes. Once when I had a chance to talk with a sales rep from Mizuno, he admitted, "Our shoes are kind of plain and don't stand out. We stand by our quality, but they aren't that attractive." I know what he's trying to say. They have no gimmicks, no sense of style, no catchy slogan. So to the average consumer, they have little appeal. (The Subaru of the shoe world, in other words.) Yet the soles of these shoes have a solid, reliable feel as you run. In my experience they're excellent partners to accompany you through twenty-six miles. The quality of shoes has gone way up in recent years, so shoes of a certain price, no matter what the maker, won't be all that much different. Still, runners sense small details that set one shoe off from another, and are always looking for this psychological edge.

I'm going to break these new shoes in, now that I have only a month left before the race.

Fatigue has built up after all this training, and I can't seem to run very fast. As I'm leisurely jogging along the Charles River, girls who look to be new Harvard freshmen keep on passing me. Most of these girls are small, slim, have on maroon Harvard-logo outfits, blond hair in a ponytail, and brand-new iPods, and they run like the wind. You can definitely feel a sort of aggressive challenge emanating from them. They seem to be used to passing people, and probably not used to being passed. They all look so bright, so healthy, attractive, and serious, brimming with self-confidence. With their long strides and strong, sharp kicks, it's easy to see that they're typical mid-distance runners, unsuited for long-distance running. They're more mentally cut out for brief runs at high speed.

Compared to them I'm pretty used to losing. There are plenty of things in this world that are way beyond me, plenty of opponents I can never beat. Not to brag, but these girls probably don't know as much as I do about pain. And, quite naturally, there might not be a need for them to know it. These random thoughts come to me as I watch their proud ponytails swinging back and forth, their aggressive strides. Keeping to my own leisurely pace, I continue my run down along the Charles.

Have I ever had such luminous days in my own life? Perhaps a few. But even if I had a long ponytail back then, I doubt if it would have swung so proudly as these girls' ponytails do. And my legs wouldn't have kicked the ground as cleanly and as powerfully as theirs. Maybe that's only to be expected. These girls are, after all, brand-new students at the one and only Harvard University.

Still, it's pretty wonderful to watch these pretty girls run. As I do, I'm struck by an obvious thought: One generation takes over from the next. This is how things are handed over in this world, so I don't feel so bad if they pass me. These girls have their own pace, their own sense of time. And I have my own pace, my own sense of time. The two are completely different, but that's the way it should be.

As I run in the morning along the river I often see the same people at the same time. One is a short Indian woman out for a stroll. She's in her sixties, I imagine, has elegant features, and is always impeccably dressed. Strangely—though maybe it's not so strange after all— she wears a different outfit every day. One time she had on an elegant sari, another time an oversize sweatshirt with a university's name on it. If memory serves, I've never seen her wearing the same outfit twice. Waiting to see what clothes she has on is one of the small pleasures of each early-morning run.

Another person I see every day is a large old Caucasian man who walks briskly with a big black brace attached to his right leg. Perhaps this was the result of some serious injury. That black brace, as far as I know, has been on for four months. What in the world happened to his leg? Whatever it is, it doesn't slow him down, and he walks at a good clip. He listens to music with some oversized headphones and silently and quickly walks down the riverside path.

Yesterday I listened to the Rolling Stones' *Beggars Banquet* as I ran. That funky "Hoo hoo" chorus in "Sympathy for the Devil" is the perfect accompaniment to running. The day before that I listened to Eric Clapton's *Reptile*. I love these albums. There's something about them that gets to me, and I never get tired of listening to them—*Reptile*, especially. Nothing beats listening to *Reptile* on a brisk morning run. It's not too brash or contrived. It has this steady rhythm and entirely natural melody. My mind gets quietly swept into the music, and my feet run in time to the beat. Sometimes, mixed in with the music coming through my headphones, I hear someone calling out, "On your left!" And a racing bike whips by, passing me on the left.

. . .

While I was running, some other thoughts on writing novels came to me. Sometimes people will ask me this: "You live such a healthy life every day, Mr. Murakami, so don't you think you'll one day find yourself unable to write novels anymore?" People don't say this much when I'm abroad, but a lot of people in Japan seem to hold the view that writing novels is an unhealthy activity, that novelists are somewhat degenerate and have to live hazardous lives in order to write. There's a widely held view that by living an unhealthy lifestyle a writer can remove himself from the profane world and attain a kind of purity that has artistic value. This idea has taken shape over a long period of time. Movies and TV dramas perpetuate this stereotypical—or, to put a positive spin on it, legendary—figure of the artist.

Basically I agree with the view that writing novels is an unhealthy type of work. When we set off to write a novel, when we use writing to create a story, like it or not a kind of toxin that lies deep down in all humanity rises to the surface. All writers have to come face-to-face with this toxin and, aware of the danger involved, discover a way to deal with it, because otherwise no creative activity in the real sense can take place. (Please excuse the strange analogy: with a fugu fish, the tastiest part is the portion near the poison—this might be something similar to what I'm getting at.) No matter how you spin it, this isn't a healthy activity.

So from the start, artistic activity contains elements

that are unhealthy and antisocial. I'll admit this. This is why among writers and other artists there are quite a few whose real lives are decadent or who pretend to be anti-social. I can understand this. Or, rather, I don't necessarily deny this phenomenon.

But those of us hoping to have long careers as professional writers have to develop an autoimmune system of our own that can resist the dangerous (in some cases lethal) toxin that resides within. Do this, and we can more efficiently dispose of even stronger toxins. In other words, we can create even more powerful narratives to deal with these. But you need a great deal of energy to create an immune system and maintain it over a long period. You have to find that energy somewhere, and where else to find it but in our own basic physical being?

Please don't misunderstand me; I'm not arguing that this is the only correct path that writers should take. Just as there are lots of types of literature, there are many types of writers, each with his own worldview. What they deal with is different, as are their goals. So there's no such thing as one right way for novelists. This goes without saying. But, frankly, if I want to write a large-scale work, increasing my strength and stamina is a must, and I believe this is something worth doing, or at least that doing it is much better than not. This is a trite observation, but as they say: If something's worth doing, it's worth giving it your best—or in some cases *beyond* your best.

To deal with something unhealthy, a person needs to be as healthy as possible. That's my motto. In other words, an unhealthy soul requires a healthy body. This might sound paradoxical, but it's something I've felt very keenly ever since I became a professional writer. The healthy and the unhealthy are not necessarily at opposite ends of the spectrum. They don't stand in opposition to each other, but rather complement each other, and in some cases even band together. Sure, many people who are on a healthy track in life think only of good health, while those who are getting unhealthy think only of that. But if you follow this sort of one-sided view, your life won't be fruitful.

Some writers who in their youth wrote wonderful, beautiful, powerful works find that when they reach a certain age exhaustion suddenly takes over. The term *literary burnout* is quite apt here. Their later works may still be beautiful, and their exhaustion might impart its own special meaning, but it's obvious these writers' creative energy is in decline. This results, I believe, from their physical energy not being able to overcome the toxin they're dealing with. The physical vitality that up till now was naturally able to overcome the toxin has passed its peak, and its effectiveness in their immune systems is gradually wearing off. When this happens it's difficult for a writer to remain intuitively creative. The balance between imaginative power and the physical abilities that sustain it has crumbled. The writer is left

employing the techniques and methods he has culti-
vated, using a kind of residual heat to mold something into what looks like a literary work—a restrained
method that can't be a very pleasant journey. Some
writers take their own lives at this point, while others
just give up writing and choose another path.

If possible, I'd like to avoid that kind of literary
burnout. My idea of literature is something more spon-
taneous, more cohesive, something with a kind of natural, positive vitality. For me, writing a novel is like
climbing a steep mountain, struggling up the face of the
cliff, reaching the summit after a long and arduous
ordeal. You overcome your limitations, or you don't,
one or the other. I always keep that inner image with me
as I write.

Needless to say, someday you're going to lose. Over
time the body inevitably deteriorates. Sooner or later,
it's defeated and disappears. When the body disinte-
grates, the spirit also (most likely) is gone too. I'm well
aware of that. However, I'd like to postpone, for as long
as I possibly can, the point where my vitality is defeated
and surpassed by the toxin. That's my aim as a novelist.
And besides, at this point I don't have the leisure to be
burned out. Which is exactly why even though people
say, "He's no artist," I keep on running.

On October 6 I'm giving a reading at MIT, and since I'll
have to speak in front of people, today as I ran I prac-

ticed the speech (not out loud, of course). When I do this, I don't listen to music. I just whisper the English in my head.

When I'm in Japan I rarely have to speak in front of people. I don't give any talks. In English, though, I've given a number of talks, and I expect that, if the opportunity arises, I'll give more in the future. It's strange, but when I have to speak in front of an audience, I find it more comfortable to use my far-from-perfect English than Japanese. I think this is because when I have to speak seriously about something in Japanese I'm overcome with the feeling of being swallowed up in a sea of words. There's an infinite number of choices for me, infinite possibilities. As a writer, Japanese and I have a tight relationship. So if I'm going to speak in front of an undefined large group of people, I grow confused and frustrated when faced by that teeming ocean of words.

With Japanese, I want to cling, as much as I can, to the act of sitting alone at my desk and writing. On this home ground of writing I can catch hold of words and context effectively, just the way I want to, and turn them into something concrete. That's my job, after all. But once I try to actually speak about things I was sure I'd pinned down, I feel very keenly that something—something very important—has spilled out and escaped. And I just can't accept that sort of disorienting estrangement.

Once I try to put together a talk in a foreign language,

though, inevitably my linguistic choices and possibilities are limited: much as I love reading books in English, speaking in English is definitely not my forte. But that makes me feel all the more comfortable giving a speech. I just think, *It's a foreign language, so what're you going to do?* This was a fascinating discovery for me. Naturally it takes a lot of time to prepare. Before I get up on stage I have to memorize a thirty- or forty-minute talk in English. If you just read a written speech as is, the whole thing will feel lifeless to the audience. I have to choose words that are easy to pronounce so people can understand me, and remember to get the audience to laugh to put them at ease. I have to convey to those listening a sense of who I am. Even if it's just for a short time, I have to get the audience on my side if I want them to listen to me. And in order to do that, I have to practice the speech over and over, which takes a lot of effort. But there's also the payoff that comes with a new challenge.

Running is a great activity to do while memorizing a speech. As, almost unconsciously, I move my legs, I line the words up in order in my mind. I measure the rhythm of the sentences, the way they'll sound. With my mind elsewhere I'm able to run for a long while, keeping up a natural speed that doesn't tire me out. Sometimes when I'm practicing a speech in my head, I catch myself making all kinds of gestures and facial expressions, and the people passing me from the opposite direction give me a weird look.

. . .

Today as I was running I saw a plump Canada goose lying dead by the shore of the Charles. A dead squirrel, too, lying next to a tree. They both looked like they were fast asleep, but they were dead. Their expressions were calm, as if they'd accepted the end of life, as if they were finally liberated. Next to the boathouse by the river was a homeless man wearing layers of filthy clothes. He was pushing a shopping cart and belting out "America the Beautiful." Whether he really meant it or was being deeply ironic, I couldn't tell.

At any rate, the calendar has changed to October. Before I know it another month will be over. And a very harsh season is just around the corner.

Six

Nobody Pounded the Table Anymore,
Nobody Threw Their Cups

Have you ever run sixty-two miles in a single day? The vast majority of people in the world (those who are sane, I should say) have never had that experience. No normal person would ever do something so foolhardy. But I did, once. I completed a race that went from morning till evening, and covered sixty-two miles. It was draining physically, as you can imagine, and for a while afterward I swore I'd never run again. I doubt I'll try it again, but who knows what the future may hold. Maybe someday, having forgotten my lesson, I'll take up the challenge of an ultramarathon

103

again. You have to wait until tomorrow to find out what tomorrow will bring.

Either way, when I look back on that race now I can see that it had a lot of meaning for me as a runner. I don't know what sort of general significance running sixty-two miles by yourself has, but as an action that deviates from the ordinary yet doesn't violate basic values, you'd expect it to afford you a special sort of self-awareness. It should add a few new elements to your inventory in understanding who you are. And as a result, your view of your life, its colors and shape, should be transformed. More or less, for better or for worse, this happened to me, and I was transformed.

What follows is based on a sketch I wrote a few days after the race, before I forgot the details. As I read these notes ten years later, all the thoughts and feelings I had that day come back in quite sharp focus. I think when you read this you'll get a general idea of what this harsh race left me with, both the happy and not-so-happy things. But maybe you'll tell me you just don't get it.

This sixty-two-mile ultramarathon takes place every year at Lake Saroma, in June, in Hokkaido. The rest of Japan is in the rainy season then, but Hokkaido is too far north. Early summer in Hokkaido is a very pleasant time of year, though in its northernmost part, where Lake Saroma is, summer warmth is still a ways off. In the early morning, when the race starts, it's still freezing, and you have to wear heavy clothes. As the sun gets higher in the sky, you gradually warm up, and the runners, like bugs going through metamorphosis, shed one layer of clothes after another. By the end of the race, though I kept my gloves on, I'd stripped down to a tank top, which left me feeling chilly. If it rained, I'd really have frozen, but fortunately, despite the lingering cloud cover, we didn't get a drop of rain.

The runners run around the shores of Lake Saroma, which faces the Sea of Okhotsk. Only once you actually run the course do you realize how ridiculously huge Lake Saroma is. Yuubetsu, a town on the west side of the lake, is the starting point, and the finish line is at Tokoro-cho (now renamed Kitami City), on the east side. The last part of the race winds through Wakka Natural Flower Garden, an extensive, long, and narrow natural arboretum that faces the sea. As courses go— assuming you can afford to take in the view—it's gorgeous. They don't control the traffic along the course, but since there aren't many cars and people to begin with, there really isn't a need to. Beside the road cows are lazily chewing grass. They show zero interest in the runners. They're too busy eating grass to care about all these whimsical people and their nonsensical activities. And for their part, the runners don't have the leisure to pay attention to what the cows are up to, either. After twenty-six miles there's a checkpoint about every six miles, and if you exceed the time limit when you pass, you're automatically disqualified. They're very strict about it, and every year a lot of runners are disqualified. After traveling all the way to the northernmost reaches of Japan to run here, I certainly don't want to get disqualified halfway through. No matter what, I'm determined to beat the posted maximum times.

This race is one of the pioneering ultramarathons in Japan, and the whole event is smoothly and efficiently run by people who live in the area. It's a pleasant event to be in.

I don't have much to say about the first part of the race, to the rest station at the thirty-fourth mile. I just ran on and on, silently. It didn't feel much different from a long Sunday-morning run. I calculated that if I could keep up a jogging pace of nine and a half minutes per mile, I'd be able to finish in ten hours. Adding in time to rest and eat, I expected to finish in under eleven hours. (Later I found out how overly optimistic I was.)

At 26.2 miles there's a sign that says, "This is the distance of a marathon." There's a white line painted on the concrete indicating the exact spot. I exaggerate only a bit when I say that the moment I straddled that line a slight shiver went through me, for this was the first time I'd ever run more than a marathon. For me this was the Strait of Gibraltar, beyond which lay an unknown sea. What lay in wait beyond this, what unknown creatures were living there, I didn't have a clue. In my own small way I felt the same fear that sailors of old must have felt.

After I passed that point, and as I was coming up on thirty-one miles, I felt a slight change physically, as if the muscles of my legs were starting to tighten up. I was hungry and thirsty, too. I'd made a mental note to remember to drink some water at every station, whether or not I felt thirsty, but even so, like an unfortunate destiny, like the dark-hearted queen of the night, thirst kept pursuing me. I felt slightly uneasy. I'd only finished half the race, and if I felt like this now, would I really be able to complete sixty-two miles?

At the rest stop at thirty-four miles I changed into fresh clothes and ate the snack my wife had prepared. Now that the sun was getting higher the temperature had risen, so I took off my half tights and changed into a clean shirt and shorts. I changed my New Balance ultra-marathon shoes (there really are such things in the world) from a size eight to an eight and a half. My feet had started to swell up, so I needed to wear shoes a half size larger. It was cloudy the whole time, with no sun getting through, so I decided to take off my hat, which I had on to keep the sun off me. I'd worn the hat to keep my head warm, too, in case it rained, but at this point it didn't look like it was going to. It was neither too hot nor too cold, ideal conditions for long-distance running. I washed down two nutrition-gel packs, took in some water, and ate some bread and butter and a cookie. I carefully did some stretching on the grass and sprayed my calves with an anti-inflammatory. I washed my face, got rid of the sweat and dirt, and used the restroom.

I must have rested about ten minutes or so, but never sat down once. If I sat down, I felt, I'd never be able to get up and start running again.

"Are you okay?" I was asked.

"I'm okay," I answered simply. That's all I could say.

After drinking water and stretching, I set out on the road again. Now it was just run and run until the finish line. As soon as I set off again, though, I realized something was wrong. My leg muscles had tightened up like a piece of old, hard rubber. I still had lots of stamina, and my breathing was regular, but my legs had a mind of their own. I had plenty of desire to run, but my legs had their own opinion about this.

I gave up on my disobedient legs and started focusing on my upper body. I swung my arms wide as I ran, making my upper body swing, transmitting the momentum to my lower body. Using that momentum, I was able to push my legs forward (after the race, though, my wrists were swollen). Naturally, you can only go at a snail's pace running like this, in a form not much different from a fast walk. But ever so slowly, as if it dawned on them again what their job was, or perhaps as if they'd resigned themselves to fate, my leg muscles began to perform normally and I was able to run pretty much the way I usually run. Thankfully.

Even though my legs were working now, the thirteen miles from the thirty-four-mile rest stop to the forty-seventh mile were excruciating. I felt like a piece of beef being run, slowly, through a meat grinder. I had the will to go ahead, but now my whole body was rebelling. It felt like a car trying to go up a slope with the parking brake on. My body felt like it was falling apart and would soon come completely undone. Out of oil, the bolts coming loose, the wrong cogs in gear, I was rapidly slowing down as one runner after another passed me. A tiny old lady around seventy or so passed me and shouted out, "Hang in there!" Man alive. What was going to happen the rest of the way? There were still twenty-five miles to go.

As I ran, different parts of my body, one after another, began to hurt. First my right thigh hurt like crazy, then that pain migrated over to my right knee, then to my left thigh, and on and on. All the parts of my body had their chance to take center stage and scream out their complaints. They screamed, complained, yelled in distress, and warned me that they weren't going to take it anymore. For them, running sixty miles was an unknown experience, and each body part had its own excuse. I understood completely, but all I wanted them to do was be quiet and keep on running. Like Danton or Robespierre eloquently attempting to persuade the dissatisfied and rebellious Revolutionary Tribunal, I tried to talk each body part into showing a little cooperation.

Encouraged them, clung to them, flattered them, scolded them, tried to buck them up. *It's just a little farther, guys. You can't give up on me now.* But if you think about it—and I did think about it—Danton and Robespierre wound up with their heads cut off.

Ultimately, using every trick in the book, I managed to grit my teeth and make it through thirteen miles of sheer torment.

I'm not a human. I'm a piece of machinery. I don't need to feel a thing. Just forge on ahead.

That's what I told myself. That's about all I thought about, and that's what got me through. If I were a living person of blood and flesh I would have collapsed from the pain. There definitely was a being called *me* right there. And accompanying that is a consciousness that is the self. But at that point, I had to force myself to think that those were convenient forms and nothing more. It's a strange way of thinking and definitely a very strange feeling—consciousness trying to deny consciousness. You have to force yourself into an inorganic place. Instinctively I realized that this was the only way to survive.

I'm not a human. I'm a piece of machinery. I don't need to feel a thing. Just forge on ahead.

I repeat this like a mantra. A literal, mechanical repetition. And I try hard to reduce the perceptible world to the narrowest parameters. All I can see is the ground three yards ahead, nothing beyond. My whole world consists of the ground three yards ahead. No need to think beyond that. The sky and wind, the grass, the cows munching the grass, the spectators, cheers, lake, novels, reality, the past, memory—these mean nothing to me. Just getting me past the next three yards—*this* was my tiny reason for living as a human. No, I'm sorry—as a *machine*.

Every three miles I stop and drink water at a water station. Every time I stop I briskly do some stretching. My muscles are as hard as week-old cafeteria bread. I can't believe these are really my muscles. At one rest stop they have pickled plums, and I eat one. I never knew a pickled plum could taste so good. The salt and sour taste spreads through my mouth and steadily permeates my entire body.

Instead of forcing myself to run, perhaps it would have been smarter if I'd walked. A lot of other runners were doing just that. Giving their legs a rest as they walked. But I didn't walk a single step. I stopped a lot to stretch, but I never walked. I didn't come here to walk. I came to run. That's the reason—the only reason—I flew all the way to the northern tip of Japan. No matter how slow I might run, I wasn't about to walk. That was the rule. Break one of my rules once, and I'm bound to break many more. And if I'd done that, it would have been next to impossible to finish this race.

While I was enduring all this, around the forty-seventh mile I felt like I'd passed through something. That's what it felt like. *Passed through* is the only way I can express it. Like my body had passed clean through a stone wall. At what exact point I felt like I'd made it through, I can't recall, but suddenly I noticed I was already on the other side. I was convinced I'd made it through. I don't know about the logic or the process or the method involved—I was simply convinced of the reality that I'd *passed through*.

After that, I didn't have to think anymore. Or, more precisely, there wasn't the need to try to consciously think about not thinking. All I had to do was go with the flow and I'd get there automatically. If I gave myself up to it, some sort of power would naturally push me forward.

Run this long, and of course it's going to be exhausting. But at this point being tired wasn't a big issue. By this time exhaustion was the status quo. My muscles were no longer a seething Revolutionary Tribunal and seemed to have given up on complaining. Nobody pounded the table anymore, nobody threw their cups. My muscles silently accepted this exhaustion now as a historical inevitability, an ineluctable outcome of the revolution. I had been transformed into a being on autopilot, whose sole purpose was to rhythmically swing his arms back and forth, move his legs forward one step at a time. I didn't think about anything. I didn't feel anything. I realized all of a sudden that even physical pain had all but vanished. Or maybe it was shoved into some unseen corner, like some ugly furniture you can't get rid of.

In this state, after I'd *passed through* this unseen barrier, I started passing a lot of other runners. Just after I crossed the checkpoint near forty-seven miles, which you had to reach in under eight hours and forty-five minutes or be disqualified, many other runners, unlike me, began to slow down, some even giving up running and starting to walk. From that point to the finish line I must have passed about two hundred. At least I counted up to two hundred. Only once or twice did somebody else pass me from behind. I could count the number of runners I'd passed, because I didn't have anything else to do. I was in the midst of deep exhaustion that I'd totally accepted, and the reality was that I was still able to continue running, and for me there was nothing more I could ask of the world.

Since I was on autopilot, if someone had told me to keep on running I might well have run beyond sixty-two miles. It's weird, but at the end I hardly knew who I was or what I was doing. This should have been a very alarming feeling, but it didn't feel that way. By then running had entered the realm of the metaphysical. First there came the action of running, and accompanying it there was this entity known as me. I run; therefore I am.

And this feeling grew particularly strong as I entered the last part of the course, the Natural Flower Garden on the long, long peninsula. It's a kind of meditative, contemplative stretch. The scenery along the coast is beautiful, and the scent of the Sea of Okhotsk wafted over me. Evening had come on (we'd started early in the morning), and the air had a special clarity to it. I could also smell the deep grass of the beginning of summer. I saw a few foxes, too, gathered in a field. They looked at us runners curiously. Thick, meaningful clouds, like something out of a nineteenth-century British landscape painting, covered the sky. There was no wind at all. Many of the other runners around me were just silently trudging toward the finish line. Being among them gave me a quiet sense of happiness. Breathe in, breathe out. My breath didn't seem ragged at all. The air calmly went inside me and then went out. My silent heart expanded and contracted, over and over, at a fixed rate. Like the bellows of a worker, my lungs faithfully brought fresh oxygen into my body. I could sense all these organs working, and distinguish each and every sound they made. Everything was working just fine. People lining the road cheered us on, saying, "Hang in there! You're almost there!" Like the crystalline air, their shouts went right through me. Their voices passed clean through me to the other side.

I'm me, *and at the same time* not *me*. That's what it felt like. A very still, quiet feeling. The mind wasn't so important. Of course, as a novelist I know that my mind is critical to doing my job. Take away the mind, and I'll never write an original story again. Still, at this point it didn't feel like my mind was important. The mind just wasn't that big a deal.

Usually when I approach the end of a marathon, all I want to do is get it over with, and finish the race as soon as possible. That's all I can think of. But as I drew near the end of this ultramarathon, I wasn't really thinking about this. The end of the race is just a temporary marker without much significance. It's the same with our lives. Just because there's an end doesn't mean existence has meaning. An end point is simply set up as a temporary marker, or perhaps as an indirect metaphor for the fleeting nature of existence. It's very philosophical—not that at this point I'm thinking how philosophical it is. I just vaguely experience this idea, not with words, but as a physical sensation.

Even so, when I reached the finish line in Tokoro-cho, I felt very happy. I'm always happy when I reach the finish line of a long-distance race, but this time it really struck me hard. I pumped my right fist into the air. The time was 4:42 p.m. Eleven hours and forty-two minutes since the start of the race.

For the first time in half a day I sat down and wiped off my sweat, drank some water, tugged off my shoes, and, as the sun went down, carefully stretched my ankles. At this point a new feeling started to well up in me—nothing as profound as a feeling of pride, but at least a certain sense of completion. A personal feeling of happiness and relief that I had accepted something risky and still had the strength to endure it. In this instance, relief outweighed happiness. It was like a tight knot inside me was gradually loosening, a knot I'd never even realized, until then, was there.

Right after this race at Lake Saroma I found it hard to walk downstairs. My legs were wobbly and I couldn't support my body well, as if my knees were about to give out. I had to hold on to the railing to walk down the stairs. After a few days, though, my legs recovered, and I could walk up and down the stairs as usual. It's clear that over many years my legs have grown used to long-distance running. The real problem, as I mentioned before, turned out to be my hands. In order to make up for my tired leg muscles, I'd vigorously pumped my hands back and forth. The day after the race my right wrist started to hurt and turned red and swollen. I'd run a lot of marathons, but this was the first time it was my arms, not my legs, that paid the greatest price.

Still, the most significant fallout from running the ultramarathon wasn't physical but mental. What I ended up with was a sense of lethargy, and before I knew it, I felt covered by a thin film, something I've sinced dubbed *runner's blues*. (Though the actual feeling of it was closer to a milky white.) After this ultramarathon I lost the enthusiasm I'd always had for the act of running itself. Fatigue was a factor, but that wasn't the only reason. The desire to run wasn't as clear as before. I don't know why, but it was undeniable: something had happened to me. Afterward, the amount of running I did, not to mention the distances I ran, noticeably declined.

After this, I still followed my usual schedule of running one full marathon per year. You can't finish a marathon if you're halfhearted about it, so I did a decent enough job of training, and did a decent enough job of finishing the races. But this never went beyond the level of *decent enough job*. It's as if loosening that knot I'd never noticed before had slackened my interest along with it. It wasn't just that my desire to run had decreased. At the same time that I'd lost something, something new had also taken root deep within me as a runner. And most likely this process of one thing exiting while another comes in had produced this unfamiliar runner's blues.

And what about this new thing within me? I can't find the exact words to describe it, but it might be something close to resignation. To exaggerate a bit, it was as if by completing the over-sixty-mile race I'd stepped into a *different place*. After my fatigue disappeared somewhere after the forty-seventh mile, my mind went into a blank state you might even call philosophical or religious. Something urged me to become more introspective, and this newfound introspection transformed my attitude toward the act of running. Maybe I no longer have the simple, positive stance I used to have, of wanting to run no matter what.

I don't know, maybe I'm making too much of it. Perhaps I'd just run too much and gotten tired. Plus I was in my late forties and was coming up against some physical barriers unavoidable for a person my age. Perhaps I was just coming to terms with the fact that I'd passed my physical peak. Or maybe I was going through a depression brought on by a sort of general male equivalent of menopause. Perhaps all these various factors had combined into a mysterious cocktail inside me. As the person involved in this, it's hard for me to analyze it objectively. Whatever it was, runner's blues was my name for it.

Mind you, completing the ultramarathon did make me extremely happy and gave me a certain amount of confidence. Even now I'm glad I ran the race. Still, I had to deal with these aftereffects somehow. For a long time after this I was in this slump—not to I imply that I had such a tremendous record to begin with, but still. Each time I ran a full marathon, my time went steadily down. Practice and racing became nothing more than formalities I went through, and they didn't move me the way they used to. The amount of adrenaline I secreted on the day of a race, too, was ratcheted back a notch. Because of this I eventually turned my focus from full marathons to triathlons and grew more enthusiastic about playing squash at the gym. My lifestyle gradually changed, and I no longer considered running the point of life. In other words, a mental gap began to develop between me and running. Just like when you lose the initial crazy feeling you have when you fall in love.

Now I feel like I'm finally getting away from the runner's-blues fog that's surrounded me for so long. Not that I've completely rid myself of it, but I can sense something beginning to stir. In the morning as I lace up my running shoes, I can catch a faint sign of something in the air, and within me. I want to take good care of this sprout that's sprung up. Just as, when I don't want to go in the wrong direction—or miss hearing a sound, miss seeing the scenery—I'm going to focus on what's going on with my body.

For the first time in a long while, I feel content running every day in preparation for the next marathon. I've opened a new notebook, unscrewed the cap on a new bottle of ink, and am writing something new. Why I feel so generous about running now, I can't really explain systematically. Maybe coming back to Cambridge and the banks of the Charles River has revived old feelings. Perhaps the warm feelings I have for this place have stirred up memories of those days when running was so central to my life. Or maybe this is simply a matter of time passing. Maybe I just had to undergo an inevitable internal adjustment, and the period needed for this to happen is finally drawing to a close.

As I suspect is true of many who write for a living, as I write I think about all sorts of things. I don't necessarily write down what I'm thinking; it's just that as I write I think about things. As I write, I arrange my thoughts. And rewriting and revising takes my thinking down even deeper paths. No matter how much I write, though, I never reach a conclusion. And no matter how much I rewrite, I never reach the destination. Even after decades of writing, the same still holds true. All I do is present a few hypotheses or paraphrase the issue. Or find an analogy between the structure of the problem and something else.

To tell the truth, I don't really understand the causes behind my runner's blues. Or why now it's beginning to fade. It's too early to explain it well. Maybe the only thing I can definitely say about it is this: That's life. Maybe the only thing we can do is accept it, without really knowing what's going on. Like taxes, the tide rising and falling, John Lennon's death, and miscalls by referees at the World Cup.

At any rate, I have the distinct feeling that time has come full circle, that a cycle has been completed. The act of running has returned as a happy, necessary part of my daily life. And recently I've been running steadily, day by day. Not as some mechanical repetition anymore, or some prescribed ceremony. My body feels a natural desire now to get out on the road and run, just like when I'm dehydrated and crave the juice from a fresh piece of fruit. I'm looking forward now to the NYC Marathon on November 6, to seeing how much I can enjoy the race, how satisfied I'll be with the run, and how I'll do.

I don't care about the time I run. I can try all I want, but I doubt I'll ever be able to run the way I used to. I'm ready to accept that. It's not one of your happier realities, but that's what happens when you get older. Just as I have my own role to play, so does time. And time does its job much more faithfully, much more accurately, than I ever do. Ever since time began (when was that, I wonder?), it's been moving ever forward without a moment's rest. And one of the privileges given to those who've avoided dying young is the blessed right to grow old. The honor of physical decline is waiting, and you have to get used to that reality.

Competing against time isn't important. What's going to be much more meaningful to me now is how much I can enjoy myself, whether I can finish twenty-six miles with a feeling of contentment. I'll enjoy and value things that can't be expressed in numbers, and I'll grope for a feeling of pride that comes from a slightly *different place*.

I'm not a young person who's focused totally on breaking records, nor an inorganic machine that goes through the motions. I'm nothing more or less than a (most likely honest) professional writer who knows his limits, who wants to hold on to his abilities and vitality for as long as possible.

One more month until the New York City Marathon.

Seven

Autumn in New York

A s if to lament the defeat of the Boston Red Sox in the playoffs (they lost every game in a Sox vs. Sox series with Chicago), for ten days afterward a cold rain fell on New England. A long autumn rain. Sometimes it rained hard, sometimes softly; sometimes, it would let up for a time like an afterthought, but not once did it clear up. From beginning to end the sky was completely covered with the thick gray clouds particular to this region. Like a dawdling person, the rain lingered for a long time, then finally made up its mind to turn into a downpour. Towns from New Hampshire to Massachusetts suffered damage from the rain, and the main highway was cut off in places. (Please understand I'm not blaming the Red Sox for all this.) I had some work to do at a college in Maine, and all I recall from the trip was driving in this gloomy rain. Except for the middle of winter, traveling in this region is usually fun, but unfortunately my trip this time wasn't very enjoyable. Too late for summer, too early for the fall colors. It was raining cats and dogs, plus the windshield wiper on my rental car was acting up, and by the time I returned to Cambridge late at night I was exhausted.

On Sunday, October 9, I ran an early-morning race, and it was still raining. This was a half marathon held every year at this time by the Boston Athletic Association, the same organization that holds the Boston Marathon in the spring. The course starts at Roberto Clemente Field, near Fenway Park, goes past Jamaica Pond, then winds back inside the Franklin Park Zoo and ends up right where it started. This year some 4,500 people participated.

I ran this race as a kind of warm-up for the New York City Marathon, so I only gave it about 80 percent, really getting fired up only in the final two miles. It's pretty hard, though, to not give it your all in a race, to try to hold back. Being surrounded by other runners is bound to have an influence on you. It's a lot of fun, after all, to be with so many fellow runners when the starters shout *Go!*, and before you know it the old competitive instinct raises its head. This time, though, I tried my best to suppress it and keep my cool: *I've got to save my energy, so I can bring it as a carry-on when I board the plane for New York.*

My time was one hour and fifty-five minutes. Not too bad, and about what I expected. The last couple of miles I floored it, passing about a hundred runners and making it to the finish line with energy to spare. The other runners around me were mainly Caucasians, especially a lot of women. For whatever reason, there weren't many minority runners. It was a cold Sunday morning, with a mistlike rain falling the entire time. But pinning a number on my back, hearing the other runners' breathing as we ran down the road, I was struck by a thought: *The racing season is upon us.* Adrenaline coursed through me. I usually run alone, so this race was a good stimulus. I got a pretty good feeling for the pace I should maintain in the marathon next month. For what will happen in the second half of that race, I'll just have to wait and see.

When I'm training I regularly run the length of a half marathon, and often much farther, so this Boston race seemed over before it began. *Is that all?* I asked myself. This was a good thing, though, since if a half marathon left me exhausted, a full marathon would be hellish.

The rain continued off and on for quite a while, and during this time I had to take a work-related trip, so I wasn't able to run as much as I'd have liked. But with the New York City Marathon fast approaching, it really isn't such a problem if I can't run. Actually, it's to my advantage to rest. The problem is, I know I should take a break and rest up, but with a race coming up I get excited and end up running anyway. If it's raining, though, I give up easily enough. I suppose that's one good side of having it rain so much.

Even though I'm not doing much running, my knee has started to hurt. Like most of the troubles in life it came on all of a sudden, without any warning. On the morning of October 17, I started to walk down the stairs in our building and my right knee suddenly buckled. When I twisted it in a certain direction the kneecap hurt in a peculiar way, a little different from an everyday ache. At a certain point it started to feel unsteady and I couldn't put any weight on it. That's what they mean by wobbly knees. I had to hold on to the railing to get downstairs.

I was exhausted from all the hard training, and most likely the sudden dip in temperature was bringing this to the surface. The summer heat still lingered in the beginning of October, but the weeklong period of rain had quickly ushered in the fall to New England. Until a short while ago I'd been using my air conditioner, but now a chilly breeze blew through the town, and you could see the signs of late autumn everywhere. I had to hurriedly drag some sweaters out of the dresser. Even the faces of the squirrels looked different as they scurried around collecting food. My body tends to have problems during these transitions from one season to another, something that never happened when I was young. The main problem is when it gets cold and damp.

If you're a long-distance runner who trains hard every day, your knees are your weak point. Every time your feet hit the ground when you run, it's a shock equivalent to three times your weight, and this repeats itself perhaps over ten thousand times a day. With the hard concrete surface of the road meeting this ridiculous amount of weight (granted, there's the cushioning of the shoes between them), your knees silently endure all this endless pounding. If you think of this (and I admit it's something I don't usually think about), it would seem strange if you *didn't* have a problem with your knees. You have to expect the knees to want to complain sometimes, to come up with a comment like, "Huffing and puffing down the road's all well and good, but how about paying attention to me every once in a while? Remember, if we go out on you, we can't be replaced."

When was the last time I gave my knees any serious thought? As I was pondering this, I started to feel a little remorseful. They're absolutely right. You can replace your breath any number of times, but not your knees. These are the only knees I'll ever have, so I'd better take good care of them.

As I said before, I've been fortunate as a runner not to have had any major injuries. And I've never had to cancel a race or drop out because of illness. Several times in the past, my right knee has felt strange (it's always the right knee), but I've always been able to soothe it and keep it going. So my knee should be okay now too, right? That's what I'd like to think. But even in bed I still feel uneasy. What'll I do if after all this I can't run in the race? Was there something wrong with my training schedule? Maybe I didn't stretch enough? (Maybe I really didn't.) Or maybe in the half marathon I ran too hard at the end? With all these thoughts running through my head I couldn't sleep well. Outside the wind was cold and noisy.

The next morning, after I woke up, washed my face, and drank a cup of coffee, I tried walking down the stairs in our apartment building. I gingerly descended the stairs, holding on to the railing and paying close attention to my right knee. The inner part of the right knee still felt strange. That's the spot where I could detect a hint of pain, though it wasn't the startling, sharp pain of the day before. I tried going up and down the stairs one more time, and this time I went down the four flights and back up again at close to normal speed. I tried all sorts of ways of walking, testing my knee by twisting it at various angles, and felt a little relieved.

This isn't connected to running, but my daily life in

Cambridge isn't going that smoothly. The building we're living in is undergoing some major remodeling, and during the day all you hear is drills and grinders. Every day is an endless procession of workmen passing by outside our fourth-story window. The construction work starts at seven thirty in the morning, when it's still a little dark outside, and continues until three thirty. They made some mistake in the drainage work on the veranda above us, and our apartment got totally wet from the rain leaking in. Rain even got our bed wet. We mobilized every pot and pan we had, but still it wasn't enough to catch all the water dripping down, so we covered the floor with newspapers. And as if this weren't enough, the boiler suddenly gave out, and we had to do without hot water and heating. But that wasn't all. Something was wrong with the smoke detector in the hall, and the alarm blared all the time. So altogether, every day was pretty noisy.

Our apartment was near Harvard Square, close enough that I could walk to the office, so it was convenient, but moving in right when they were doing major remodeling was a bit of bad luck. Still, I can't spend all my time complaining. I've got work to do, and the marathon's fast approaching.

Long story short: my knee seems to have settled down, which is definitely good news. I'm going to try to be optimistic about things.

. . .

There's one more piece of good news. My public reading at MIT on October 6 went very well. Maybe even *too* well. The university had prepared a classroom that had a 450-person capacity, but about 1,700 people poured in, which meant that most had to be turned away. The campus police were called in to straighten things out. Due to the confusion the reading started late, and on top of that the air conditioner wasn't working. It was as hot as midsummer, and everyone in the room was dripping with sweat.

"Thank you all very much for taking the time to attend my reading," I began. "If I'd known there would be this many attending I would have booked Fenway Park." Everyone was hot and irritated by the confusion, and I thought it best to try to get them to laugh. I took off my jacket and gave my reading wearing a T-shirt. The audience's reaction was great—most of them were students—and from start to finish I could enjoy myself. It made me really happy to see so many young people interested in my novels.

One other project I'm involved in now is translating Scott Fitzgerald's *The Great Gatsby*, and things are going well. I've finished the first draft and am revising the second. I'm taking my time, going over each line carefully, and as I do so the translation gets smoother and I'm better able to render Fitzgerald's prose into more natural Japanese. It's a little strange, perhaps, to make this claim at such a late date, but *Gatsby* really is an outstanding novel. I never get tired of it, no matter how many times I read it. It's the kind of literature that nourishes you as you read, and every time I do I'm struck by something new, and experience a fresh reaction to it. I find it amazing how such a young writer, only twenty-nine at the time, could grasp—so insightfully, so equitably, and so warmly—the realities of life. How was this possible? The more I think about it, and the more I read the novel, the more mysterious it all is.

On October 20, after resting and not running for four days because of the rain and that weird sensation in my knee, I ran again. In the afternoon, after the temperature had risen a bit, I put on warm clothes and slowly jogged for about forty minutes. Thankfully, my knee felt all right. I jogged slowly at first, but then gradually sped up when I saw things were going okay. Everything was okay, and my leg, knee, and heel were working fine. This was a great relief, because the most important thing for me right now is running in the New York City Marathon and finishing it. Reaching the finish line, never walking, and enjoying the race. These three, in this order, are my goals.

The sunny weather continued for three days straight, and the workers were finally able to finish the drainage work on the roof. As David, the tall young construction foreman from Switzerland, had told me—a dark look on his face as he glanced up at the sky—they could finish the work only if it was sunny for three days in a row, and finally it was. No more worrying about leaks anymore. And the boiler's been fixed and we have hot water again, so I can finally take a hot shower. The basement had been off-limits during the repairs, but now we can go down there and use the washer and dryer again. They tell me that tomorrow the central heating will come on. So, after all these disasters, things—including my knee—are finally taking a turn for the better.

October 27. Today I was finally able to run at about 80 percent without any strange sensations in my knee. Yesterday I still felt something weird, but this morning I can run normally. I ran for fifty minutes, and for the last ten minutes picked up the pace to the speed I'll have to have when I actually run the NYC Marathon. I pictured entering Central Park and getting near the finish line, and it was no problem at all. My feet hit the pavement hard, and my knees didn't buckle. The danger is over. Probably.

It's become really cold, and the town is full of Halloween pumpkins. In the morning the path along the river is lined with wet, colorful fallen leaves. If you want to run in the morning, gloves are a must.

October 29, the marathon a week away. In the morning it started snowing off and on, and by the afternoon it was a full-scale snowfall. *Summer wasn't all that long ago*, I thought, impressed. This was typical New England weather. Out the window of my campus office I watched the wet snowflakes falling. My physical condition isn't too bad. When I get too tired from training, my legs tend to get heavy and my running is unsteady, but these days I feel light as I start off. My legs aren't so tired anymore, and I feel like I want to run even more.

Still, I feel a bit uneasy. Has the dark shadow really disappeared? Or is it inside me, concealed, waiting for its chance to reappear? Like a clever thief hidden inside a house, breathing quietly, waiting until everyone's asleep. I have looked deep inside myself, trying to detect something that might be there. But just as our consciousness is a maze, so too is our body. Everywhere you turn there's darkness, and a blind spot. Everywhere you find silent hints, everywhere a surprise is waiting for you.

All I have to go on are experience and instinct. Experience has taught me this: *You've done everything you needed to do, and there's no sense in rehashing it. All you can do now is wait for the race.* And what instinct has taught me is one thing only: *Use your imagination.* So I close my eyes and see it all. I imagine myself, along with thousands of other runners, going through Brooklyn, through Harlem, through the streets of New York. I see myself crossing several steel suspension bridges, and experience the emotions I'll have as I run along bustling Central Park South, close to the finish line. I see the old steakhouse near our hotel where we'll eat after the race. These scenes give my body a quiet vitality. I no longer fix my gaze on the shades of darkness. I no longer listen to the echoes of silence.

Liz, who looks after my books at Knopf, sends me an e-mail. She's also going to run the New York City Marathon, in what will be her first full marathon. "Have a good time!" I e-mail back. And that's right: for a marathon to mean anything, it *should* be fun. Otherwise, why would thousands of people run 26.2 miles?

I check on the reservation at our hotel on Central Park South and buy our plane tickets from Boston to New York. I pack my running outfit and shoes, which I've broken in pretty well, in a gym bag. Now all that's left is to rest and wait for the day of the race. All I can do is pray that we have good weather, that it's a gorgeous autumn day.

Every time I visit New York to run the marathon (this will be the fourth time) I remember the beautiful, smart ballad by Vernon Duke, "Autumn in New York."

> *It's autumn in New York*
> *It's good to live it again.*

New York in November really does have a special charm to it. The air is clear and crisp, and the leaves on the trees in Central Park are just beginning to turn golden. The sky is so clear you can see forever, and the skyscrapers lavishly reflect the sun's rays. You feel you can keep on walking one block after another without end. Expensive cashmere coats fill the windows at Bergdorf Goodman, and the streets are filled with the delicious smell of roasted pretzels.

On the day of the race, as I run those very streets, will I be able to fully enjoy this *autumn in New York*? Or will I be too preoccupied? I won't know until I actually start running. If there's one hard and fast rule about marathons, it's that.

Eight

18 Til I Die

Right now I'm training for a triathlon. Recently I've been focusing on bicycle training, pedaling hard one or two hours a day down a bicycle path along the seaside at Oiso called the Pacific Oceanside Bicycle Path, the wind whipping at me from the side. (Belying its wonderful name, the path is narrow and even cut off at various points, and not easy to ride on.) Thanks to all this perilous training, my muscles from my thighs to my lower back are tight and strong.

The bike I use in races is the kind with toe straps that let you push down on the pedals *and* lift. Doing both increases your speed. In order to keep the motion of your legs smooth, it's important to focus on the lifting part, especially when you're going up a long slope. The problem is, the muscles you use for lifting those pedals are hardly ever used in daily life, so when I really get into bike training these muscles inevitably get stiff and exhausted. But if I train on the bike in the morning, I can run in the evening, even though my leg muscles are stiff. I wouldn't call this kind of practice fun, but I'm not complaining. This is exactly what I'll be facing in the triathlon.

Running and swimming I like to do anyway, even if I'm not training for a race. They're a natural part of my daily routine, but bicycling isn't. One reason I'm reluctant when it comes to bicycling is that a bike's a kind of tool. You need a helmet, bike shoes, and all sorts of other accoutrements, and you have to maintain all the parts and equipment. I'm just not very good at taking care of tools. Plus, you have to find a safe course where you can pedal as fast as you want. It always seems like too much of a hassle.

The other factor is fear. To get to a decent bike path I have to ride through town, and the fear I feel when I weave in and out of traffic on my sports bike with its skinny tires and my bike shoes strapped tight in the straps is something you can't understand unless you've gone through it. As I've gotten more experienced I've gotten used to it, or at least learned how to survive, but there have been many moments startling enough to put me in a cold sweat.

Even when I'm practicing, whenever I go into a tight curve fast my heart starts pounding. Unless I keep the right trajectory and lean my body at exactly the correct angle as I go into the curve, I'll fall over or crash into a fence. Experientially I've had to find the limits I can take my speed to. It's pretty scary, too, to be going down a slope at a good clip when the road's wet from the rain. In a race one little mistake is all it takes to cause a massive pileup.

I'm basically not a very nimble person and don't like sports that rely on speed combined with agility, so bicycling is definitely not my forte. That's why, among the three parts of a triathlon—swimming, bicycling, and running—I always put off practicing bicycling till last. It's my weakest link. Even if I excel in the running part of the triathlon, the 6.2 miles, that final segment is never long enough to make up the time. This is exactly why I decided I had to take the plunge and put in some quality time on the bike. Today is August 1 and the race is on October 1, so I have exactly two months. I'm not sure I'll be able to build up my biking muscles in time, but at least I'll get used to the bike again.

The one I'm using now is a light-as-a-feather Panasonic titanium sports bike, which I've been using for the last seven years. Changing the gears is like one of my own bodily functions. It's a wonderful machine. At least the machine is superior to the person riding it. I've ridden it pretty hard in four triathlons but never had any major problem. On the body of the bike is written "18 Til I Die," the name of a Bryan Adams hit. It's a joke, of course. Being eighteen until you die means you die when you're eighteen.

The weather's been strange in Japan this summer. The rainy season, which usually winds down in the beginning of July, continued until the end of the month. It rained so much I got sick of it. There were torrential rains in parts of the country, and a lot of people died. They say it's all because of global warming. Maybe it is, and maybe it isn't. Some experts claim it is, some claim it isn't. There's some proof that it is, some that it isn't. But still people say that most of the problems the earth is facing are, more or less, due to global warming. When sales of apparel go down, when tons of driftwood wash up on the shore, when there are floods and droughts, when consumer prices go up, most of the fault is ascribed to global warming. What the world needs is a set villain that people can point at and say, "It's all your fault!"

At any rate, due to this villain that can't be dealt with, it went on raining, and I could hardly practice biking at all during July. It's not my fault—it's that villain's. Finally, though, these last few days have been sunny and I've been able to take my bike outdoors. I strap on my streamlined helmet, put on my sports sunglasses, fill my bottle with water, set my speedometer, and take off.

The first thing to remember when you ride a competitive bike is to lean forward as much as possible to be more aerodynamic—especially to keep your face forward and up. No matter what, you have to learn this pose. Until you're used to it, holding in this position for over an hour—like a praying mantis with a raised head—is next to impossible. Very quickly your back and neck start to scream. When you get exhausted your head tends to drop and you look down, and once that happens all the dangers lurking out there strike.

When I was training for my first triathlon and rode nearly sixty-two miles at a stretch, I ran right into a metal post—one of those stakes set up to prevent cars and motorcycles from using the recreational lane along a river. I was tired, my mind elsewhere, and I neglected to keep my face forward. The front wheel of the bike got all bent out of shape, and I was flung head first to the ground. I suddenly found myself literally flying through the air. Fortunately, my helmet protected my head; otherwise I would have been badly injured. My arms were scraped pretty badly against the concrete, but I was lucky to get away with just that. I know a few other cyclists who've suffered injuries much worse.

Once you have a scary incident like that, you really take it to heart. In most cases learning something essential in life requires physical pain. Since that incident on the bike, no matter how tired I might be I always keep my head up and my eyes on the road ahead.

Naturally all this attention taxes my overworked

muscles, but even in this August heat I'm not sweating. Actually, I probably am, but the strong headwind makes it evaporate. Instead, I'm thirsty. If I leave it too long I'll get dehydrated, and if that happens my mind will get all blurry. I never go cycling without a water bottle. As I'm cycling along, I take the bottle from its rack, gulp down some water, and return it. I've trained myself to do this series of actions smoothly, automatically, always making sure to face forward.

When I first began I had no idea what I was doing, so I asked a person who knows a lot about bike racing to coach me. On holidays the two of us would load our bikes in a station wagon and set out for Oi Pier. Delivery trucks don't come to the pier on holidays, and the wide road that goes past all the warehouses makes a fantastic cycling course. A lot of cyclists gather there. The two of us would decide how many circuits we'd make, in how long, and set off. He accompanied me on long-distance rides—the kind I got into an accident on—as well.

Cycling training alone is, truthfully, pretty tough. Long runs done to prepare for marathons are definitely lonely, but hanging on to the handlebars of a bike all by yourself and pedaling on and on is a much more solitary undertaking. It's the same movements repeated over and over. You go up slopes, on level ground, and down slopes. Sometimes the wind's with you, sometimes against you. You switch gears as needed, change your position, check your speed, pedal harder, let up a bit, check your speed, drink water, change gears, change your position . . . Sometimes it strikes me as an intricate form of torture. In his book the triathlete Dave Scott wrote that of all the sports man has invented, cycling has got to be the most unpleasant of all. I totally agree.

Still, in the few months before the triathlon, no matter how illogical it may be, this is what I must do. Desperately humming the riff from "18 Til I Die," sometimes cursing the world, I push down on the pedals, pull up on them, forcing my legs to remember the right rhythm. A hot wind from the Pacific rushes past, grazing my cheeks and making them sting.

My time at Harvard was over at the end of June, which meant the end of my stay in Cambridge. (Farewell, Sam Adams draft beer! Good-bye, Dunkin' Donuts!) I gathered all my luggage together and returned to Japan at the beginning of July. What were the main things I did while in Cambridge? Basically, I confess, I bought a ton of LPs. In the Boston area there are still a lot of high-quality used record stores. When I had the time I also checked out record stores in New York and Maine. Seventy percent of the records I bought were jazz, the rest classical, plus a few rock records. I'm a very (or perhaps I should say *extremely*) enthusiastic record collector. Shipping all these records back to Japan was no mean feat.

I'm not really sure how many records I have in my home right now. I've never counted them, and it's too scary to try. Ever since I was fifteen I've bought a huge number of records, and gotten rid of a huge number. The turnover is so fast I can't keep track of the total. They come, they go. But the total number of records is most definitely increasing. The number, though, is not the issue. If somebody asks me how many records I have, all I can say is, "Seems like I have a whole lot. But still not enough."

In Scott Fitzgerald's *The Great Gatsby*, one of the characters, Tom Buchanan, a rich man who's also a well-known polo player, says, "I've heard of making a garage out of a stable, but I'm the first man who ever made a stable out of a garage." Not to brag, but I'm doing the same thing. Whenever I find a quality LP recording of a piece I have on CD, I don't hesitate to sell the CD and buy the LP. And when I find a better-quality recording, something closer to the original, I don't hesitate to trade in the old LP for a new one. It takes a lot of time to pursue this, not to mention a considerable investment of cash. Most people would, I am pretty sure, label me obsessed.

As planned, in November 2005 I ran the New York City Marathon. It was a beautiful, sunny autumn day, the kind of wonderful day when you expect to see the late Mel Tormé appear out of nowhere, leaning against a grand piano as he croons out a verse from "Autumn in

New York." That morning, along with tens of thousands of other runners, I started the race at the Verrazano Narrows Bridge on Staten Island; moved through Brooklyn, where the writer Mary Morris is always waiting to cheer me on; then, through Queens; through Harlem and the Bronx; and several hours and bridges later arrived at the finish line, near the Tavern on the Green in Central Park.

And how was my time? Truth be told, not so great. At least, not as good as I'd been secretly hoping for. If possible, I was hoping to be able to wind up this book with a powerful statement like, "Thanks to all the hard training I did, I was able to post a great time at the New York City Marathon. When I finished I was really moved," and casually stroll off into the sunset with the theme song from *Rocky* blaring in the background. Until I actually ran the race I still clung to the hope that things would turn out that way, and was looking forward to this dramatic finale. That was my Plan A. A really great plan, I figured.

But in real life things don't go so smoothly. At certain points in our lives, when we really need a clear-cut solution, the person who knocks at our door is, more likely than not, a messenger bearing bad news. It isn't always the case, but from experience I'd say the gloomy reports far outnumber the others. The messenger touches his hand to his cap and looks apologetic, but that does nothing to improve the contents of the message. It isn't the messenger's fault. No good to blame him, no good to grab him by the collar and shake him. The messenger is just conscientiously doing the job his boss assigned him. And this boss? That would be none other than our old friend Reality.

Before the race I was in great shape, I thought, and well rested. The strange sensation I'd had on the inside of my knee had vanished. My legs, especially around my calves, still felt a bit tired, but it wasn't something I needed to worry about (or so I thought). My training schedule had gone smoothly, better than for any other race before. So I had this hope (or moderate conviction) that I'd post the best time I'd run in recent years. All I needed to do now was cash in my chips.

At the start line I followed the pace leader with the 3 HOURS 45 MINUTES placard. I was sure I could definitely make that time. That might have been a mistake. Looking back on it, I should have followed the three-hour-and-fifty-five-minute pace leader, and picked up the pace later, and only if I was sure I could handle it. That sort of sensible approach was probably what I needed. But something else was pushing me on: *You practiced as hard as you could in all that heat, didn't you? If you can't make this time, then what's the point? You're a man, aren't you? Start acting like one!* This voice whispered in my ear, just like the voices of the cunning cat and fox that tempted Pinocchio on his way to school. Up until not too long ago a time of three hours and forty-five minutes had been, for me, just business as usual.

Up to mile sixteen I was able to keep up with the pace leader, but after that it was impossible. It was hard to admit this to myself, but gradually my legs wouldn't move, so my speed started to fall off. The 3 HOURS 50 MINUTES banner passed me by. This was the worst possible scenario. No matter what, I couldn't let the four-hour pace leader pass me. After I crossed the Madison Avenue Bridge and started down the wide, straight path from Uptown to Central Park, I began to feel a little better and had a faint hope that I was getting back on track, but this was short lived, for right when I entered Central Park and was facing the infamous gradual slope, I started getting a cramp in my right calf. It wasn't so awful that I had to stop, but the pain forced me to run at nearly a walking pace. The crowd around me kept urging me on, shouting, "Go! Go!," and I wanted nothing more than to keep on running, but I couldn't control my legs anymore.

So in the end I missed the four-hour mark by just a little. I did complete the run, after a fashion, which means I maintained my record of completing every marathon I've been in (a total of twenty-four now). I was able to do the bare minimum, but it was a frustrating result after all my hard training and meticulous planning. It felt like a remnant of a dark cloud had wormed its way into my stomach. No matter what, I couldn't accept this. I'd trained so hard, so why did I get cramps? I'm not trying to argue that all effort is fairly rewarded, but if there is a God in heaven, was it asking too much to let me glimpse a sign? Was it too much to expect a little kindness?

About a half year later, in April 2006, I ran the Boston Marathon. As a rule I run only one marathon a year, but since the New York City Marathon left such a bad taste in my mouth I decided to give it another try. This time, though, I intentionally, and drastically, reduced the amount of training I did. Training hard for New York hadn't helped much. Maybe I'd done *too much* training. This time I didn't set a schedule, but instead just ran a bit more than usual every day, keeping my mind clear of abstruse thoughts, doing only what I felt like. I tried to have a casual attitude. It's only a marathon, I told myself. I decided to just go with this and see what happened.

This was my seventh time running the Boston Marathon, so I knew the course well—how many slopes there were, what all the curves were like—not that this guaranteed I'd do a good job.

So, you're asking, what was the result?

My time wasn't much different from New York. Having learned my lesson there, I'd tried my best to keep things under control during the first half of the Boston race, maintaining my pace, holding some energy in reserve. I enjoyed running, watching the scenery go by, waiting for the point where I felt I could pick it up a notch. But that point never came. From mile twenty to mile twenty-two, the point where you pass Heartbreak Hill, I felt fine. No problem at all. My friends who were waiting at Heartbreak Hill to cheer me on later on said, "Haruki looks really good." I ran up the hill smiling and waving. I was sure that at this rate I could pick up the pace and run a decent time. But after I passed Cleveland Circle and entered downtown Boston, my legs started to get heavy. Very quickly exhaustion overtook me. I didn't get cramps, but in the last few miles of the race, after passing over Boston University Bridge, it was all I could do not to get left behind. Picking up the pace like I'd planned was impossible.

I was able to finish, of course. Under the partly cloudy sky I ran the full 26.2 miles without stopping and slipped past the finish line, which was set up in front of the Prudential Center. I wrapped myself in a silver thermal sheet to ward off the cold, and received a medal from one of the volunteers. A wave of relief washed over me — relief that I didn't have to run anymore. It always feels wonderful to finish a marathon — it's a beautiful achievement — but I wasn't satisfied with the time. Usually I look forward to a cold Sam Adams draft beer after a race, but now I didn't even feel like having one. Exhaustion had seeped into each and every organ.

"What in the world happened?" My wife, who had been waiting for me at the finish line, was baffled. "You're still pretty strong, and I know you train enough."

What indeed? I wondered, not having a clue. Maybe I'm simply getting older. Or perhaps the reason lies elsewhere, maybe something critical I've overlooked. At this point, anyway, any speculation has to remain just that: speculation. Like a small channel of water silently being sucked up into the desert.

There's one thing, though, I can state with confidence: until the feeling that I've done a good job in a race returns, I'm going to keep running marathons, and not let it get me down. Even when I grow old and feeble, when people warn me it's about time to throw in the towel, I won't care. As long as my body allows, I'll keep on running. Even if my time gets worse, I'll keep on putting in as much effort—perhaps even *more* effort—toward my goal of finishing a marathon. I don't care what others say—that's just my nature, the way I am. Like scorpions sting, cicadas cling to trees, salmon swim upstream to where they were born, and wild ducks mate for life.

I may not hear the *Rocky* theme song, or see the sunset anywhere, but for me, and for this book, this may be a sort of conclusion. An understated, rainy-day-sneakers sort of conclusion. An anticlimax, if you will. Turn it into a screenplay, and the Hollywood producer would just glance at the last page and toss it back. But the long and the short of it is that this kind of conclusion fits who I am.

What I mean is, I didn't start running because somebody asked me to become a runner. Just like I didn't become a novelist because someone asked me to. One day, out of the blue, I wanted to write a novel. And one day, out of the blue, I started to run—simply because I wanted to. I've always done whatever I felt like doing in life. People may try to stop me, and convince me I'm wrong, but I won't change.

I look up at the sky, wondering if I'll catch a glimpse of kindness there, but I don't. All I see are indifferent summer clouds drifting over the Pacific. And they have nothing to say to me. Clouds are always taciturn. I probably shouldn't be looking up at them. What I should be looking at is inside of me. Like staring down into a deep well. Can I see kindness there? No, all I see is my own nature. My own individual, stubborn, uncooperative, often self-centered nature that still doubts itself—that, when troubles occur, tries to find something funny, or something nearly funny, about the situation. I've carried this character around like an old suitcase, down a long, dusty path. I'm not carrying it because I like it. The contents are too heavy, and it looks crummy, fraying in spots. I've carried it with me because there was nothing else I was supposed to carry. Still, I guess I have grown attached to it. As you might expect.

· · ·

So here I am training every day for the Murakami City Triathlon in Niigata Prefecture. In other words, I'm still lugging around that old suitcase, most likely headed toward another anticlimax. Toward a taciturn, unadorned maturity — or, to put it more modestly, toward an evolving dead end.

Nine

At Least He Never Walked

Once when I was around sixteen and nobody else was home, I stripped naked, stood in front of a large mirror in our house, and checked out my body from top to bottom. As I did this I made a mental list of all the deficiencies—or what, to me at least, appeared to be deficiencies. For instance (and these are just instances), my eyebrows were too thick, or my fingernails were shaped funny—that sort of thing. As I recall, when I got to twenty-seven items, I got sick of it and gave up. And this is what I thought: *If there are this many visible parts of my body that are worse than normal people's, then if I start considering other aspects—personality, brains, athleticism, things of this sort—the list will be endless.*

Sixteen is an intensely troublesome age. You worry about little things, can't pinpoint where you are in any objective way, become really proficient at strange, pointless skills, and are held in thrall by inexplicable complexes. As you get older, though, through trial and error you learn to get what you need, and throw out what should be discarded. And you start to recognize (or be resigned to the fact) that since your faults and deficiencies are well nigh infinite, you'd best figure out your good points and learn to get by with what you have.

But this wretched sort of feeling I had as I stood in front of the mirror at sixteen, listing all my physical shortcomings, is still a sort of touchstone for me even now. The sad spreadsheet of my life that reveals how much my debts far outweigh my assets.

Now, some forty years later, as I stand at the seashore in a black swimsuit, goggles on top of my head, waiting for the start of the triathlon, this memory of so long ago suddenly comes back to me. And once more I'm struck by how pitiful and pointless this little container called *me* is, what a lame, shabby being I am. I feel like everything I've ever done in life has been a total waste. In a few minutes I'm going to swim .93 miles, ride a bike 24.8 miles, then run a final 6.2 miles. And what's all that sup-

posed to prove? How is this any different from pouring
water in an old pan with a tiny hole in the bottom?

Well, at least it's a beautiful, perfect day—perfect
weather for a triathlon. No wind, not a wave in the sea.
The sun's bathing the ground in warmth, the temperature at about 73 degrees. The water is ideal. This is the
fourth time I've taken part in the triathlon in Murakami
City in Niigata Prefecture, and all the previous years the
conditions have been atrocious. Once the sea was too
rough, as the Japan Sea in the fall is apt to be, so we had
to substitute a beach run for the swimming portion.
Even when conditions weren't so drastic, I'd have all
kinds of awful experiences: it would rain, or the waves
would be so high I couldn't breathe well when I did the
crawl, or else it'd be so cold I'd freeze on the bike. In
fact, whenever I drive the 217 miles to Niigata for this
triathlon I'm always expecting the worst in terms of
weather, convinced that something terrible's going to
happen. It might as well be a sort of image training
for me. Even this time, when I first saw the placid,
warm sea, I felt like someone was trying to pull a fast
one. *Don't fall for it,* I warned myself. This was just
make-believe; there had to be a trap lying in wait.
Maybe a school of vicious, poisonous jellyfish. Or a pre-
hibernation, ravenous bear would charge at my bike. Or
an unfortunate bolt of lightning would zap me right in
the head. Or maybe I'd be attacked by a swarm of angry
bees. Maybe my wife, waiting for me at the finish line,

was going to have discovered some awful secrets about me (I suddenly felt like there might actually be some). Needless to say, I always view this meet, the Murakami International Triathlon, with a bit of trepidation. I never have any idea what will happen.

No doubt about it now, though, today the weather's great. As I stand here in my rubber suit, I'm actually starting to get warm.

Around me are people dressed the same way, all fidgeting as they wait for the race to start. A weird scene, if you think about it. We're like a bunch of pitiful dolphins washed up on the shore, waiting for the tide to come in. Everyone else looks more upbeat about the race than I am. Or maybe it just looks that way. Anyway, I've decided to keep my mind clear of the extraneous. I've traveled all this way, and now I have to do my best to get through the race. For three hours all I need to do is keep my mind blank and just swim, ride a bike, and run.

When are we going to start? I check my watch. But it's only a short time after the last time I checked it. Once the race begins I won't, ideally, have any time to think . . .

Up to this point I've been in six triathlons of various lengths, though for four years, from 2001 to 2004, I didn't participate in any. The blank in my record exists because during the 2000 Murakami Triathlon I suddenly found myself unable to swim and was disqualified. It's taken some time to get over the shock and regain my composure. It wasn't at all clear to me why I couldn't swim. I mulled over various possibilities in my mind, and as I did so my confidence took a nosedive. I'd been in many races, but this was the first time I'd ever been on the Disqualified roster.

Truthfully, this wasn't the first time I'd stumbled during the swimming portion of a triathlon. In the pool or in the ocean I'm able to do the crawl over a long distance without pushing it. Usually I can swim 1,500 meters (a swimmer's mile) in about thirty-three minutes—not especially fast, but good enough for a triathlon. I grew up near the sea and am used to ocean swimming. Some people who practice only in pools find it hard, and frightening, to swim in the ocean, but not me. I actually find it easier because there's so much space and you're more buoyant.

For some reason, though, whenever it comes down to an actual race, I blow the swimming portion. Even when I entered the relatively short-distance Tinman competition, in Oahu, Hawaii, I couldn't do the crawl very well. I got into the water, got ready to swim, and suddenly had trouble breathing. I'd lift my head to breathe, same as always, but the timing was off. And when I'm not breathing right, fear takes over and my muscles tense up. My chest starts pounding, and my arms and legs won't move the way I want them to.

I get scared to put my face in the water and start to panic.

In the Tinman competition, the swimming portion is shorter than usual, at only half a mile, so I was able to give up on the crawl and switch to the breaststroke. But in a regular 1,500-meter race you can't get by swimming the breaststroke. It's slower than the crawl, and at the end your legs are exhausted. So in the Murakami Triathlon in 2000 the only thing left for me was to tearfully be disqualified.

I got out and went up on shore, but felt so mad at myself that I got back in the water and tried swimming the course over again. The other participants had long since finished the swimming portion and had set off on their bikes, so I was swimming all alone. And this time I was able to do the crawl with no problem. I could breathe easily and move my body smoothly. So why couldn't I swim like this during the race?

At the first triathlon I'd ever participated in there was a floating start, where all the participants lined up in the water. As we were waiting, the person next to me kicked me hard in the side several times. It's a competition, so it's to be expected—everybody's trying to get ahead of others and take the shortest route. Getting hit in the elbow while you're swimming, getting kicked, swallowing water, having your goggles fall off—it's all par for the course. But for me, getting kicked hard like that in my first race was a shock, and that may have thrown my swimming off. Perhaps subconsciously that memory was coming back to me every time I started a race. I don't want to think that way, but the mental side of a race is critical, so it's very possible.

Another problem was that there was something wrong with the way I was swimming. My crawl was self-taught, and I've never had a coach. I could swim as long as I cared to, but nobody would ever have said I have an economical or beautiful form. Basically it was the kind of swimming where I just gave it all I had. For a long time I'd been thinking that if I was going to get serious about triathlons I'd have to do something to improve my swimming. Along with searching for what went wrong on the mental side, I figured it wouldn't be a bad idea to work on my form. If I could improve the technical side of my swimming, other issues might come into sharper focus as well.

So I put my triathlon challenge on hold for four years. During that time I kept up my usual long-distance running and ran in one marathon per year. But somehow I just wasn't happy. My failure in the triathlon accounted for part of this. *Some day*, I thought, *I'm going to get revenge*. When it comes to things like this, I'm pretty tenacious. If there's something I can't do but want to, I won't relax until I'm able to do it.

I hired a few swimming coaches to help me improve my form, but none of them were what I was looking for.

Lots of people know how to swim, but those who can efficiently teach how to swim are few and far between. That's the feeling I get. It's difficult to teach how to write novels (at least I know *I* couldn't), but teaching swimming is just as hard. And this isn't just confined to swimming and novels. Of course there are teachers who can teach a set subject, in a set order, using predetermined phrases, but there aren't many who can adjust their teaching to the abilities and tendencies of their pupils and explain things in their own individual way. Maybe hardly any at all.

I wasted the first two years trying to find a good coach. Each new coach tinkered with my form just enough to mess up my swimming, sometimes to the point where I could hardly swim at all. Naturally, my confidence went down the drain. At this rate there was no way I could enter a triathlon.

Things started to improve around the time I realized that revolutionizing my form was probably impossible. My wife was the one who found me a good coach. She'd never been able to swim her whole life, but she happened to meet a young woman coach at the gym she's a member of, and you wouldn't believe how well she swims now. She recommended that I try this young woman as my coach too.

The first thing this coach did was check my overall swimming and ask what my goals were. "I want to participate in a triathlon," I told her. "So you want to be able to do the crawl in the ocean and swim long distances?" she asked. "That's right," I replied. "I don't need to sprint over short distances." "Good," she said. "I'm glad you have clear-cut goals. That makes it easier for me."

So we began one-on-one lessons to reshape my form. Her approach wasn't a slash-and-burn policy, totally dismissing the way I've been swimming up till now and rebuilding from the ground up. I imagine that for an instructor it's much more difficult to reshape someone's form who's already able, after a fashion, to swim, than to start with a nonswimmer, a blank sheet. It isn't easy to get rid of bad swimming habits, so my new coach didn't try to forcefully do a total makeover. Instead, she revised very small movements I made, one by one, over an extended period of time.

What's special about this woman's teaching style is that she doesn't teach you the textbook form at the beginning. Take body rotation, for instance. To get her pupil to learn the correct way, she starts out by teaching how to swim *without* any rotation. In other words, people who are self-taught in the crawl have a tendency to be overconscious of rotation. Because of this there's too much resistance in the water and their speed goes down—plus, they waste energy. So in the beginning, she teaches you to swim like a flat board without any body rotation—in other words, completely the opposite of what the textbook says. Needless to say, when I swam that way I felt like an awful, awkward swimmer. As I practiced persistently, I could swim the way she told me to, in this awkward way, but I wasn't convinced it was doing any good.

And then, ever so slowly, my coach started to add some rotation. Not emphasizing that we were practicing rotation, but just teaching a separate way of moving. The pupil has no idea what the real point of this sort of practice is. He merely does as he's told, and keeps on moving that one part of his body. For example, if it's how to turn your shoulders, you just repeat that endlessly. Sometimes you spend an entire session just turning your shoulders. You end up exhausted and spent, but later, in retrospect, you realize what it all was for. The parts fall into place, and you can see the whole picture and finally understand the role each individual part plays. The dawn comes, the sky grows light, and the colors and shapes of the roofs of houses, which you could only glimpse vaguely before, come into focus.

This might be similar to practicing drumming. You're made to practice bass drum patterns only, day after day. Then you spend days on just the cymbals. Then just the tom tom . . . Monotonous and boring for sure, but once it all falls together you get a solid rhythm. In order to get there you have to stubbornly, rigorously, and very patiently tighten all the screws of each individual part. This takes time, of course, but sometimes taking time is actually a shortcut. This is the path I followed in swimming, and after a year and a half I was able to swim long distances far more gracefully and efficiently than ever before.

And while I was training for swimming, I made an important discovery. I had trouble breathing during a race because I'd been hyperventilating. The same exact thing happened when I was swimming in the pool with my coach, and it dawned on me: just before the start of the race I was breathing too deeply and quickly. Probably because I was tense before a race, I got too much oxygen all at once. This led to me breathing too fast when I started to swim, which in turn threw off the timing of my breathing.

It was a tremendous relief when I finally pinpointed the real problem. All I had to do now was make sure not to hyperventilate. Now before a race starts I get into the sea, swim a bit, and get my body and mind used to swimming in the ocean. I breathe moderately in order not to hyperventilate, and breathe with my hand over my mouth in order not to get too much oxygen. "I'm all set now," I tell myself. "I've changed my form, and am no longer the swimmer I used to be."

And so, in 2004, for the first time in four years, I again entered the Murakami Triathlon. A siren marked the start, everyone began swimming, and somebody kicked me in the side. Startled, I was afraid that once again I was going to mess up. I swallowed some water, and the thought crossed my mind that I should switch to the breaststroke for a while. But my courage returned, and I told myself that there was no need for that, that things would work out. My breathing calmed down, and I started the crawl again. I concentrated not on breathing in, but on breathing out in the water. And I heard that nice old sound of my exhalations bubbling underwater. *I'm okay now*, I told myself as I neatly rode the waves.

Happily, I was able to conquer my panic and finish the triathlon. I hadn't been in one for so long, and hadn't had time to do bicycle training, so my overall time wasn't much to speak of. But I was able to achieve my first goal: wiping away the shame of being disqualified. As usual, my main feeling was one of relief.

I'd always thought I was sort of a brazen person, but this issue with hyperventilating made me realize a part of me was, unexpectedly, high strung. I had no idea how nervous I got at the start of a race. But it turns out I really was tense, just like everybody else. It doesn't matter how old I get, but as long as I continue to live I'll always discover something new about myself. No matter how long you stand there examining yourself naked before a mirror, you'll never see reflected what's inside.

And here I am again, at nine thirty a.m. on October 1, 2006, a sunny fall Sunday, standing once more on the shores of Murakami City in Niigata Prefecture, waiting for the triathlon to begin. A little nervous, but making sure not to hyperventilate. I go over my mental checklist one more time, just to be certain I haven't forgotten anything. Computerized ankle bracelet—*check*. I've rubbed Vaseline all over my body so when I finish swimming I can easily get my wetsuit off. I've carefully done my stretching. I've drunk enough water. And used the toilet. Nothing left to do. I hope.

I've been in this race a few times, so I recognize a few of the other participants. As we wait for the race to start, we shake hands and chat. I'm not the type who gets along easily with others, but for some reason with other triathletes I have no problem. Those of us who participate in triathlons are unusual people. Think about it for a minute. Most all the participants have jobs and families, and on top of taking care of these, they swim and bike and run, training very hard, as part of their ordinary routine. Naturally this takes a lot of time and effort. The world, with its commonsensical viewpoint, thinks their lifestyle is peculiar. And it would be hard to argue with anyone who labeled them eccentrics and oddballs. But there's something we share, not something as exaggerated as solidarity, perhaps, but at least a sort of warm emotion, like a vague, faintly colored mist over a late-spring peak. Of course, competition is part of the mix—it's a race, after all—but for most of the people participating in a triathlon the competitive aspect is less important than the sense of a triathlon as a sort of ceremony by which we can affirm this shared bond.

In this sense, the Murakami Triathlon is a convenient race. There aren't so many competitors (somewhere between three hundred and four hundred), and the race is run in a very low-key way. It's a small, local, homemade type of triathlon. The people in the town warmly support us. There's nothing gaudy or overdone about the race, and that quiet kind of atmosphere appeals to me. Apart from the race itself, there are wonderful hot springs nearby, the food is great, and the local sake (especially Shimehari Tsuru) is outstanding. Over the years that I've participated in the race, I've made some acquaintances in the area. There are even people who come all the way from Tokyo to cheer me on.

At 9:56 the start siren goes off, and everyone immediately begins the crawl. This is it—the most nerve-racking moment of all.

I plunge in and start kicking and plowing through the water with my arms. I try to clear my mind of everything extraneous and concentrate not on inhaling, but on exhaling. My heart's pounding, and I can't get the rhythm right. My body's a bit stiff. And as you might expect, somebody kicks me in the shoulder again. Somebody else is leaning over me, getting on top of my back, like one turtle getting on top of another. I swallow some water, but not very much. *Nothing to worry about*, I tell myself. *Don't panic.* I breathe in and out at a steady rhythm, and that's the most critical thing right now. As I do, the tension drains away. Things are going to be okay. Just keep swimming like this. Once I get the rhythm down, all I have to do is maintain it.

But then—and with triathlons you almost expect this—some unforeseen trouble leaps out at me. As I'm doing the crawl I raise my head to check my direction and think *What the . . . ?* My goggles are all fogged up, and I can't see a thing . . . It's like the whole world is cloudy and opaque. I stop swimming, tread water, and rub the goggles with my fingers to try to clear them up. But still I can't see. What is going on? The goggles are a pair I use all the time, and I've done a lot of training with them so I can see where I'm going as I swim. So what in the world is happening? Then it hits me. After I rubbed my skin with Vaseline I didn't wash my hands, so I wiped the goggles with oily fingers. What an asinine thing to do! At the start line I always wipe my goggles with saliva, which keeps the inside from fogging up. And this time I had to go and forget to do that.

During the whole 1,500-meter swim my foggy goggles bothered me. I was constantly off course, swimming in the wrong direction, and wasted a lot of time. Sometimes I had to stop, remove my goggles, tread water, and figure out where I should go. Imagine a blindfolded child trying to hit a piñata, and you get the idea.

If I'd thought about it, I could have swum without my goggles. I should have just taken them off. When I was swimming, however, I was kind of confused and didn't have the presence of mind to figure that out. Thanks to this, the swimming part of the race was pretty disorderly, and my time wasn't nearly as good as what I'd been hoping for. In terms of my ability—remember how hard I'd trained for this—I should have been able to swim much faster. I consoled myself with the thought that at least I wasn't disqualified, didn't get left behind that much, and was able to finish the swim. And whenever I managed to swim in a straight line, I did a decent job of it, I think.

I got up on the beach and made straight for where the bikes were parked (which seems easy but actually isn't), peeled off my snug wetsuit, tugged on my bike shoes and helmet and wraparound sunglasses, gulped down some water, and, finally, headed out onto the road. I was able to do all that so mechanically that by the time I was thinking again, I realized I'd been splashing around in the water until just a minute before and now was whizzing by at twenty miles an hour on a bike. No matter how many times I experience this, the sudden transition feels odd. It's a different feeling of weight, speed, and motor reflexes, and you use completely different muscles. You feel like a salamander that's evolved overnight into an ostrich. My brain wasn't able to make the switch very quickly, and neither could my body. I couldn't keep the pace up, and before I knew it seven other racers had passed me. *This isn't good*, I thought, and up to the turning point I didn't pass anyone.

The bike segment follows a well-known stretch of seacoast called Sasagawa Nagare. It's a very scenic spot, with unusual rock formations jutting out of the water, though of course I didn't have the time to enjoy the scenery. We raced from Murakami City northward along the sea, with the turn near the border with Yamagata Prefecture that would send us back along the same road. There were slopes in several places, but nothing steep enough to make me blank out. Before reaching the turn, I didn't worry about passing others or being passed, but focused instead on pedaling at a steady pace, using an easy gear. At regular intervals I'd reach down for my water bottle and grab a quick drink. As I did all this I gradually started to feel comfortable on the bike again. Feeling I could handle it now, when we reached the turn I downshifted, sped up, and in the second half of the race passed seven people. The wind wasn't blowing hard, so I could pedal for all I was worth. When the wind's strong, amateur bicyclists like me get pretty dejected. Making the wind work for you takes years of experience and a great deal of skill. When there's no wind, though, it all comes down to a question of leg strength. I wound up finishing the 24.8 miles at a faster clip than I'd expected, then tugged on my good old running shoes for the final leg of the race.

When I switched to running, though, things got pretty rough. Normally I would have held back a little in the bike portion to save up energy for the run, but this time, for whatever reason, it just didn't cross my mind. I just let 'er rip, then plunged right into running. As you can imagine, my legs didn't work right. My mind ordered them, "Run!," but my leg muscles were on strike. I could see myself running but had no sensation of running.

Each race is a little different, but the same basic thing happens every triathlon. The muscles I've pushed hard for over an hour while biking, the ones I still want to be open for business when I start running, just won't move smoothly. It takes time for the muscles to change from one rail to another. For the first two miles both my legs always seem locked up, and only after that am I finally able to *run*. This time, though, it took a lot longer to get to this point. Of the three events in a triathlon, running is obviously my specialty, and usually I'm able to easily pass at least thirty other runners. But this time I could only pass ten or fifteen. Still, I was glad to be able to even out my performance a bit. In my last triathlon I'd been passed by a lot of people in the bike portion, but this time it was my run time that wasn't so great. Even so, the difference between the events I was good at and those I wasn't had decreased, meaning that perhaps I was getting the hang of being a true triathlete. This was definitely something to cheer about.

As I ran through the beautiful old part of Murakami City, the cheers of the spectators—ordinary residents,

I'm assuming—spurred me on, and I wrung out my last ounce of energy as I raced for the finish line. It was an exultant moment. It had been a tough race, for sure, what with my Vaseline adventure, but once I reached the finish that all vanished. After I caught my breath, I exchanged a smile and a handshake with the man wearing race number 329. "Good job," we told each other. He and I had battled it out in the bike race, where he passed me many times. Right when we started running, my shoelaces came untied and twice I had to stop to retie them. If only that hadn't happened, I know I would have passed him—or so goes my optimistic hypothesis. When I picked up the pace at the end of the run, I almost passed him, but wound up three yards short. Naturally the responsibility for not checking my shoelaces before the race lies entirely with yours truly.

At any rate, I'd happily made it to the finish line set up in front of the Murakami City Hall. The race was over. I didn't drown, didn't get a flat, didn't get stung by a vicious jellyfish. No ferocious bear hurled himself at me, and I wasn't stung by wasps, or hit by lightning. And my wife, waiting at the finish line, didn't discover some unpleasant truth about me. Instead, she greeted me with a smile. Thank goodness.

The happiest thing for me about this day's race was that I was able, on a personal level, to truly enjoy the

event. The overall time I posted wasn't anything to brag
about, and I made a lot of little mistakes along the way.
But I did give it my best, and I felt a nice, tangible after-
glow. I also think I've improved in a lot of areas since the
previous race, which is an important point to consider.
In a triathlon the transition from one event to the next
is difficult, and experience counts for everything.
Through experience you learn how to compensate for
your physical shortcomings. To put it another way,
learning from experience is what makes the triathlon so
much fun.

Of course it was painful, and there were times when,
emotionally, I just wanted to chuck it all. But pain
seems to be a precondition for this kind of sport. If pain
weren't involved, who in the world would ever go to
the trouble of taking part in sports like the triathlon or
the marathon, which demand such an investment of
time and energy? It's precisely because of the pain,
precisely because we want to overcome that pain, that
we can get the feeling, through this process, of really
being *alive* — or at least a partial sense of it. Your quality
of experience is based not on standards such as time
or ranking, but on finally awakening to an awareness
of the fluidity within action itself. If things go well,
that is.

On the way back to Tokyo from Niigata I saw quite a
few cars with bicycles strapped to their roofs on their
way back from the race. The people inside were all

tanned and strong looking—the typical triathlon physique. After our unpretentious race on a fall Sunday, we were all on our way back to our own homes, back to our own mundane lives. And with the next race in mind, each of us, in our place, will most likely silently go about our usual training. Even if, seen from the outside, or from some higher vantage point, this sort of life looks pointless or futile, or even extremely inefficient, it doesn't bother me. Maybe it's some pointless act like, as I've said before, pouring water into an old pan that has a hole in the bottom, but at least the effort you put into it remains. Whether it's good for anything or not, cool or totally uncool, in the final analysis what's most important is what you can't see but can feel in your heart. To be able to grasp something of value, sometimes you have to perform seemingly inefficient acts. But even activities that appear fruitless don't necessarily end up so. That's the feeling I have, as someone who's felt this, who's experienced it.

I have no idea whether I can actually keep this cycle of inefficient activities going forever. But I've done it so persistently over such a long time, and without getting terribly sick of it, that I think I'll try to keep going as long as I can. Long-distance running (more or less, for better or worse) has molded me into the person I am today, and I'm hoping it will remain a part of my life for as long as possible. I'll be happy if running and I can grow old together. There may not seem to be much logic to it, but it's the life I've chosen for myself. Not that, at this late date, I have other options.

These thoughts went through my head as I drove along after the triathlon, headed for home.

I expect that this winter I'll run another marathon somewhere in the world. And I'm sure come next summer I'll be out in another triathlon somewhere, giving it my best shot. Thus the seasons come and go, and the years pass by. I'll age one more year, and probably finish another novel. One by one, I'll face the tasks before me and complete them as best I can. Focusing on each stride forward, but at the same time taking a long-range view, scanning the scenery as far ahead as I can. I am, after all, a long-distance runner.

My time, the rank I attain, my outward appearance — all of these are secondary. For a runner like me, what's really important is reaching the goal I set myself, under my own power. I give it everything I have, endure what needs enduring, and am able, in my own way, to be satisfied. From out of the failures and joys I always try to come away having grasped a concrete lesson. (It's got to be concrete, no matter how small it is.) And I hope that, over time, as one race follows another, in the end I'll reach a place I'm content with. Or maybe just catch a glimpse of it. (Yes, that's a more appropriate way of putting it.)

Some day, if I have a gravestone and I'm able to pick out what's carved on it, I'd like it to say this:

Haruki Murakami
1949–20**
Writer (and Runner)
At Least He Never Walked

At this point, that's what I'd like it to say.

Afterword

On Roads All Round the World

A s the headings of each chapter of this book indicate, the bulk of the writings collected here were composed between the summer of 2005 and the fall of 2006. I didn't write them at one stretch, but rather a little at a time, whenever I could find free time in between other work. Each time I wrote more I'd ask myself, *So—what's on my mind right now?* Though this isn't a long book, it took quite some time from beginning to end, and even more after I'd finished, to carefully polish and rework it.

Over the years, I've published a number of essay collections and travel writings, but I haven't had much opportunity like this to focus on one theme and write directly about myself, so I was scrupulous about making sure it was exactly the way I wanted it. I didn't want to write too much about myself, but if I didn't honestly talk about what needed to be said, writing this book would have been pointless. I needed to revisit the manuscript many times over a period of time; otherwise I wouldn't have been able to explore these delicate layers.

I see this book as a kind of memoir. Not something as grand as a personal history, but calling it an essay collection is a bit forced. This is repeating what I said in the foreword, but through the act of writing I wanted to sort out what kind of life I've led, both as a novelist and as an ordinary person, over these past twenty-five years. When it comes to the question of how much a novelist should stick to the novel, and how much he should reveal his real voice, everyone will have his own standard, so it's impossible to generalize. But for me, there was the hope that writing this book would allow me to discover my own personal standard. I'm not very confident that I've done a good job in this area. Still, when I finished, I had the feeling that a weight had been lifted. (I think it may have been just the right moment to write this book when I did.)

After I finished, I took part in several races. I'd been planning to participate in a marathon in Japan at the beginning of 2007, but just before the race, unusually for me, I caught a cold and couldn't run. If I had run, it would have been my twenty-sixth marathon. As a result,

I reached the end of the season—which ran from the fall of 2006 through the spring of 2007—without running a single marathon. I feel a little regretful, but will try my best next season.

Instead of a marathon, in May I participated in the Honolulu Triathlon, an Olympic-length event. I could finish it easily and really enjoy myself, and ended with a better time than the last. And at the end of July I was in the Tinman Triathlon, also held in Honolulu. Because I was living there for about a year, I also took part in a kind of triathlon training camp, practicing with other Honolulu residents three times a week for three months. This kind of training program really helped, and I was able to make some "Triath buddies" in the group.

Running a marathon during the cold months and taking part in a triathlon during the summer has become the cycle of my life. There's no off-season, so I always seem to be busy, but I'm not about to complain. It's brought me a lot of happiness. Truthfully, I am sort of interested in trying a full-scale triathlon like the Ironman competition, but if I went that far I'm afraid the training would (most definitely) take so much time out of my schedule it would interfere with my real job. I didn't pursue more ultramarathons for the same reason. For me, the main goal of exercising is to maintain, and improve, my physical condition in order to keep on writing novels, so if races and training cut into the time I need to write, this would be putting the cart before the horse. Which is why I've tried to maintain a decent balance.

Meanwhile, running for a quarter century makes for a lot of good memories.

One I remember in particular was running, in Central Park in 1983, with the writer John Irving. I was translating his novel *Setting Free the Bears* at the time, and while I was in New York I asked to interview him. He told me he was busy but if I'd come in the morning while he jogged in Central Park we could talk while we ran together. We talked about all kinds of things as we jogged around the park early one morning. Naturally I didn't tape our conversation and couldn't take any notes, so all that I recall now is the happy memory of the two of us jogging together in the brisk morning air.

In the 1980s I used to jog every morning in Tokyo and often passed a very attractive young woman. We passed each other jogging for several years and got to recognize each other by sight and smile a greeting each time we passed. I never spoke to her (I'm too shy), and of course don't even know her name. But seeing her face every morning as I ran was one of life's small pleasures. Without pleasures like that, it's pretty hard to get up and go jogging every morning.

One other memory I hold dear is running high up in Boulder, Colorado, with Yuko Arimori, the Japanese silver medalist in the marathon at the Barcelona Olympics. This was just some light jogging, but still, coming from Japan and running all of a sudden at a height of ten thousand feet was very tough—my lungs screamed, and I felt dizzy and terribly thirsty. Miss Arimori gave me a cool look and just said, "Is something the matter, Mr. Murakami?" I learned how rigorous the world of professional runners is (though I should add that she's a very kind person). By the third day, though, my body had gotten used to the thin atmosphere, and I could enjoy the crisp air of the Rockies.

I've met many people through running, which has been one of its real pleasures. And many people have helped me, and encouraged me. At this point what I should do—like in an Academy Awards acceptance speech—is express my thanks to many people, but there are too many to thank, and the names would probably mean nothing to most readers. I'll confine myself to the following.

The title of this book is taken from the title of a short-story collection by a writer beloved to me, Raymond Carver, *What We Talk About When We Talk About Love*. I'm thankful to his widow, Tess Gallagher, who was kind enough to give me permission to use the title in this way. I am also deeply thankful to the editor of this book, Midori Oka, who has patiently waited for ten years.

Finally, I dedicate this book to all the runners I've encountered on the road—those I've passed, and those who've passed me. Without all of you, I never would have kept on running.

HARUKI MURAKAMI
AUGUST 2007

www.vintage-books.co.uk